THE END OF TYRANNY

HOPE AT THE END OF THE AGE

JOHN J. BLANCHARD
Great Lakes Church of God

"This book is dedicated to the Family of Man."

John J. Blanchard

Acknowledgements

This book would not have been possible without the support and encouragement of the members of the Great Lakes Church of God. Though small in number, their faith in God and love for humanity inspired me to complete the book you now hold. Volunteers were always available to share the burdens of typing, transcribing, and editing.

Several dear friends from outside our Church congregation gave unselfishly of their time to make this a better book. Their constructive criticism was invaluable and much appreciated.

To all who helped, I extend my sincerest thanks.

John J. Blanchard

Table of Contents

Introduction

To billions of people the Bible is known as the "good book" and God as a loving Being, someone to turn to in the hour of need. Almost anyone who believes in God holds that faith in Him is well placed. Ultimately faith in God should result in a sense of calm amidst the storms, an assurance that all will be well. Most of the world believes in a Supreme Being, so why is there so much anxiety today?

Governments around the world are desperately trying to restore stability to their crumbling economies. Veritable mountains of money are being thrown at a growing list of bewildering problems. Dollars, euros, pounds, yen, yuan, rubles, and rupees have been and are being spent. Brilliant economists, outstanding businessmen, successful investors, and political leaders offer up proposals, ideas, and potential solutions to the problems. Many of the suggestions are excellent: better laws and regulation, more transparency, stimulus plans, and debt relief, to name a few. So far all these noble efforts have not halted the downward spiral. There is a very simple and fundamental reason why. Too many people have lost hope in the future.

Sentiment around the world has changed. The unbridled optimism of just a few years ago that spawned hope has been dashed. The world was talking about achieving truly great things. Plans were being implemented to wipe out malaria, turn back the tide of HIV-AIDs, and bring the world out of poverty. Indeed in the last twenty-five years more people have risen out of poverty than in the history of the world. Free trade was lifting all the world's boats. More and more people were living in freedom with one human rights victory after another. In a matter of months everything has unraveled as if we knew deep inside that it was all too good to be true.

Embedded deep within the human race are the nagging feelings of doubt and guilt. Around the world cultures, faiths, and traditions have held that the end of the world would be very ugly indeed. Leaders in government and business are fighting a tide of despair, born of deeply held religious conviction. How do you fight that? What is the antidote to the poison injected into the human race by the avalanche of bad news? What is the antidote to the incredible special effects that depict the end on television and in movies? What is the antidote to the flood of books, supposedly based on Scripture, that depict a horrible end for all but a lucky few at the hands of an angry and vengeful God?

The antidote is to prove them all wrong by using God's very own words. The antidote is to use the Bible to expose error and misunderstanding. Within the Bible is God's plan to spare mankind from the long-awaited doom. To the contrary of what most of us have been taught, the end of the world is a great time to be alive! Mankind's best days lie just ahead. The nations and peoples of this beleaguered planet are about to experience something wonderful and grand! What you see around you – our cities, towns, and villages, our forests, rivers, oceans, and mountains – are about to enter the long-awaited Millennium. The Millennium is a thousand-year period that will get better, cleaner, and more beautiful with each passing day. Money, stimulus plans, and better laws are good things, but without hope for a better future, they have nothing solid to build on. God's plan provides that solid foundation, a foundation upon which hope is well placed. As Abraham Lincoln once said, "The power of hope upon human exertion and happiness is wonderful." That power is just getting started, and when it has its full head of steam, the sentiment of despair will disappear like the shroud of fog at the dawn of a sunny day!

We face many vexing problems today, but that has been mankind's lot for 6,000 years. There seems to be one crisis after another. There really is one huge difference today. The God who created the family of man and loves us all is about to liberate the human race. He has spent six millenia preparing to deliver the human race from the tyranny that has been the source of our misery. Mankind's best days are truly just ahead.

1

The Current Distress Among Nations

What a confusing time this is to be alive! The drumbeat of bad news is absolutely fearful. It seems there is no escaping the dreadful noise that bombards us daily, and what a depressing exercise it has become to keep informed on the latest developments of world news. Every day this noise grows louder as the world and its inhabitants cope with economic turmoil, business failures, huge financial bailouts, corrupt political leaders in many nations, housing foreclosures, unemployment, recession, depression, genocide, terrorism, weapons of mass destruction, global warming, natural disasters, and unstable governments wielding nuclear power.

How does one deal with the feelings of futility, anxiety, and helplessness at a time when the future looks so bleak? For many it may feel as if mankind has been caught in a powerful current that is relentlessly and mercilessly drawing us toward the brink of a precipice, with the expectation that we will drop to our destruction.

News reports today are often delivered in language containing serious spiritual overtones. Words and phrases such as "apocalyptic," "of Biblical proportions," and "Armageddon" are bandied about with a general understanding among the populace that these mean doom and gloom on the horizon. Bad news is often made even more disturbing through the analysis of many evangelists and theologians who interpret every major event through the lens of "end-time prophetic warnings." If they are to be believed, then we can only conclude that the vast majority of us are doomed to destruction, with God as the causal agent behind it all. The question on many minds today is, have we been abandoned by a supreme God to fall to a horrible end, whether we deserve it or not? Biblical history makes it evident enough that the only thing worse than being abandoned by God is to have Him turn against us in His wrath.

Where are we *really* going from here? Who has the right answers? Do we have the ability to recognize true answers if we found them? And what do we do next? Do we just wait it out and hope for the best? Is there any message of hope for human beings, anywhere? In this book, we will explore the answers to these questions, looking to the only source we have available to us to gain any kind of insight into what an All-Powerful Creator God Being has to say about us, about our times, and about our future. Though millions scoff at the notion that the Bible contains anything more than myths, fables, and legends connected to a detached God, millions more genuinely seek substance and meaning for their lives from these words recorded in ancient times. Is God still involved with His creation, and is He about to emerge front and center into the lives of all men and women on Earth? Are the changes predicted to come upon this earth wrapped in horror for the majority of mankind, or are there other pieces to this puzzle to be considered and understood?

In this book we are going to search out together what the Bible actually says about our time today, and we will seek straight answers to our questions regarding the "end of the world." Can we as individuals find out for ourselves what God intends for the human race? We will search Scripture for answers to such questions as:
- Is God at war with the human race?
- Are we truly in the last days?
- What is "the Great Tribulation?"
- What is "Armageddon?"
- Who or what are the four horsemen of the apocalypse?
- What is "the Millennium?"
- How can we hear God's voice?
- How can we understand God's symbolic language?
- How can we understand the meaning of end-time prophecies?
- What is "prophetic time?"
- What does God expect of us?

Answers to these questions will bring us inner peace and confidence toward the future. We must make a determination within ourselves to see beyond the evening news and the gloomy rhetoric. Challenge the doomsday crowd and prove they are wrong. Seek confidence to go on living life with hope and positive expectation. It is time to shine the light of truth, to find out just what the Bible says that truth is, to counter those who trade in fear by using God's name to support their predictions.

Truth, understanding, and the application of it in our reasoning can only free us from deception and allow us greater insight into God and His purpose for us. The history of the struggles and developments of mankind show us that knowledge unshackles the mind to go on to ever greater discovery and invention. This book is not meant to disrespect or offend anyone or to attack any particular set of beliefs. This is meant to be a book of discovery, coming to a greater understanding of the Book that has mystified men and women throughout the ages. Seek the validity and depth of the Book we call the word of God, the Holy Bible. There is indeed a very loving and all-powerful Creator God who is dynamically working to bring about the greatest age for man that has yet to see the light of day!

2

A Calm Look at "The End of the World"

The Bible has so much to say about the present time in which we live that it is difficult to know where to start. Perhaps the best place to begin is to determine what God means by the phrase "end of the world" and what He said would be the most common misconceptions regarding this event.

The most often quoted prophecy regarding the latter days is what is commonly referred to as the "Olivet Prophecy." Three gospels, Matthew, Mark, and Luke, contain this discourse, with each one contributing pertinent information.

Matthew 24:1-2 opens with Christ and His disciples departing from the temple in Jerusalem, heading toward the Mount of Olives located east of the city: "Then Jesus went out and departed from the temple, and His disciples came up to show Him the buildings of the temple. And Jesus said to them, 'Do you not see all these things? Assuredly, I say to you, not one stone shall be left here upon another, that shall not be thrown down.'" The prophecy begins when they reach the Mount of Olives and the disciples ask Christ two very straight-forward questions in verse 3: "'Tell us when will these things be? And what will be the sign of Your coming, and of the end of the age?'" Right here is where many people were set off the rails by earlier translations such as the very widely distributed King James Version. The phrase "end of the age" was poorly translated as "end of the world." By implication "end of the world" conjures up visions of a final destructive climax rather than a transition to a new age. The ancient Greek word *aion* is defined as "an age" (#165 Strong 1995). What is being discussed in these verses is the return of Christ with the accompanying signs. Inherent in Christ's return are many positive changes for the earth and mankind.

To make absolutely certain that people would not be confused by the signs that would lead up to and accompany His return, Christ told the apostles what *not* to heed. His startling answer begins in verse 4: "And Jesus answered and said to them: 'Take heed that no one deceives you. For many will come in My name, saying, "I am the Christ," and will deceive many.'" The warning is that many would come representing Him, and will deceive many by what they say. Christ goes on to tell us what they will be saying. "'And you will hear of wars and rumors of wars. See that you are not troubled; for all these things must come to pass, but the end is not yet. ["End" is the Greek word *telos* (#5056 Strong 1995), as in telescope and means the final, long-term goal or conclusion.] For nation will rise against nation, and kingdom against kingdom. And there will be famines, pestilences, and earthquakes in various places. All of these are the beginning of sorrows.'" "Beginning of sorrows" is *arche* (#746 Strong 1995), and *odin* (#5604 Strong 1995), in ancient Greek. Taken together, these words signify the chief pains and sorrows toward birth. "Beginning of sorrows" is better stated as the main sorrows and birth pangs you will experience on the way toward the end of the age. Therefore Christ was warning not to be duped by those who would be pointing to various calamities and catastrophes down through time as signs associated with His coming, and signs of the end. Further into the chapter in verse 24 He strengthened His warning by adding, "'False christs and false prophets will rise and show great signs and wonders to deceive...'" "Signs and wonders" in the ancient Greek is *semeion* (#4592 Strong 1995) and *teras* (#5059 Strong 1995), meaning supernatural markers and omens used as indicators. Christ again made it very clear that many would come in His name claiming that specific wars, famines, earthquakes, disease and other disasters were being orchestrated by Christ as supernatural signs of His imminent return. Untold thousands today as well as those in the distant past have done just that. It is impossible to calculate the damage that has been done by turning people's attention from the true signs and wonders that have occurred along the way and are occurring at this very time.

Some of these signs are mentioned in Matthew 24: the abomination of desolation, tribulation, signs in the heavens, and the budding of a fig tree. Before we tackle the meaning of these fascinating signs and wonders, we must become conversant with God's prophetic language and symbolism. Bear in mind what Christ just told us: catastrophic death and destruction are not going to accompany His return. We will close the chapter with an incident in Luke 9:51-56 that proves this point. In verses 51-54 it is told how a Samaritan village had been insulting to Christ. The disciples became angry and wanted Christ to call down fire to destroy the village. Christ's response starts in verse 55: "But He turned to them and rebuked them, and said, 'You do not know what manner of spirit you are of. For the Son of Man did not come to destroy men's lives but to save them.'" God's spirit wants to save and heal, but there is a cruel spirit whose purpose is to destroy – the same spirit behind the false signs and wonders. Exposing his deception weakens his power dramatically.

There is nothing more fascinating than the study of God's true signs and wonders at this critical time in history.

3
Comprehending Biblical Mystery and Symbolism

God had to inspire the Bible in such a way that it would have relevancy to every generation, from the time the first book was penned by Moses, until the apostle John wrote the final book, Revelation. The Bible was written over a span of fifteen centuries, with the last chapter written almost 2,000 years ago. These pages contain information that is general in nature that can benefit anyone at any time. They also contain many messages and information for people alive at specific times far into the future from the time the words were written. This required God to conceal much information that He could reveal at the right moment in time.

Hidden information to be revealed later is called "prophecy" in the way most people understand the term. Prophecy can also mean simply inspired teaching, depending on context. God employs many devices to conceal prophetic information. Among them are confusing numbers, dates, mysterious symbolism, and riddles that are also called parables. These devices are often overlapped and intertwined to form an unbreakable enigma. Taken together these devices form a type of language. If you know the language, you can then discern God's thoughts. God controls how much of this language He wants understood at any given time.

Without God's inspiration, any human attempt to understand prophecy and figure things out ends up a fiasco. Misunderstanding God's word will eventually make an adherent or group look foolish and irrelevant. This is at the very least. At the worst, such misunderstandings lead to wars, bigotry, racism, genocide, and a whole host of societal ills. Therefore it is important to "get it right."

The prophets themselves, though under the inspiration of God, often were unaware of the full extent of the meaning of their writings. Take the prophet Daniel, for example. After recording a long prophecy, he had this exchange with an angel in Daniel 12 verses 8-10: "Although I heard, I did not understand. Then I said, 'My lord, what shall be the end of these things?' And he said, 'Go your way, Daniel, for the words are closed up and sealed till the time of the end. Many shall be purified, made white, and refined, but the wicked shall do wickedly; and none of the wicked shall understand, but the wise shall understand.'" Therefore Daniel's prophecy would be revealed to the wise in the last days of the age. Those who are wise are those who are willing to consider, be circumspect, and are desirous of understanding the truth.

Any good book that we might pick off the shelf has a beginning that leads to an end. By the end, a well written book will have clearly explained what the author was trying to convey. So it is with the Bible. The last book in the Bible has the greatest concentration of mysterious symbolism and confusing language. Revelation is a prime example of how God can so completely conceal knowledge until He wants it understood. It is also a prime example of how God has given us the tools to understand it, once He shows us how to use them.

Using Revelation to Introduce God's Methods

Just mentioning the Book of Revelation conjures up images of the four horsemen of the Apocalypse, the battle of Armageddon, death, destruction, and tribulation. Hundreds of millions, perhaps billions, of people feel we have entered the final days of planet earth. They assume the signs are all around us – war, famine, pestilence, disease, earthquakes, and tsunamis. An anxious planet waits expectantly for the horrible demise we have been told that we deserve as God vents His wrath. Is this what the Bible actually says will happen? Are the multitudes of troubles and crises building to a climax that only a very special few will miraculously survive? The purpose of this book is to challenge the assumptions and foregone conclusions that rob the masses of hope yet make a smug few feel falsely secure.

The Book of Revelation contains the final chapter of a very long narrative. It is therefore a conclusion of sorts, but every conclusion must be accompanied by a beginning. The first chapters of the Bible narrative are in the Book of Genesis, which literally means "beginning." However, for anyone reading the Bible, Genesis and Revelation seem to have almost nothing in common.

The title "Revelation" is derived from the Greek *apokalupsis* (#602 Strong 1995), from which we get the English word "Apocalypse." Revelation is what *apokalupsis* means: to reveal or uncover the hidden or unknown. There is nothing more fearful to humans than the unknown.

Two things make the Book of Revelation confusing and fearful to contemplate. Firstly, this book seems somehow disconnected from the rest of the Bible. Secondly, the book abounds with God's extensive use of prophetic mystery and symbolism with their often-violent overtones. For these reasons, even avid readers of the Bible shy away from this book and are content to let Bible scholars interpret it for them. To date, their interpretations only confirm and compound our fears, leading us to await our fate with a sense of doom and resignation. These private interpretations are a large part of the problem. We would do well to heed the words of Peter regarding Scripture and its interpretation: "For we did not follow cunningly devised fables when we made known to you the power and coming of our Lord Jesus Christ, but were eyewitnesses of His majesty. For He received from God the Father honor and glory when such a voice came from the Excellent Glory: 'This is my beloved Son, in whom I am well pleased.' And we heard this voice which came from heaven when we were with Him on the holy mountain. And so we have the prophetic word confirmed, which you do well to heed as a light that shines in a dark place, until the day dawns and the morning star rises in your hearts; knowing this first, that no prophecy of Scripture is of any private interpretation, for prophecy never came by the will of man, but holy men of God spoke as they were moved by the Holy Spirit" (II Peter 1:16-21). Since there can be no private or personal interpretation of Scripture, only God Himself can reveal His thoughts.

It is not the Scriptures themselves which are suspect, as we are told in II Timothy 3 verses 16-17: "All Scripture is given by inspiration of God, and is profitable for doctrine, for reproof, for correction, for instruction in righteousness, that the man of God may be complete..." Inspiration of God means "God-breathed" in the Greek. Just as we exhale air to form words, God's divine breath, or wind, spoke the words that the apostles and prophets penned in the Bible. God's intellect is so powerful that only He can help us discern His thoughts. It becomes a question of how to use God's scriptural thoughts to interpret God's scriptural thoughts. Scripture must be used to interpret Scripture. Because this is a fundamental principle in gaining knowledge and wisdom, we will liberally employ Scripture in this book. Rather than be intimidated, we will find the Bible to be the most interesting book we have ever held in our hands. We are going to use educational principles outlined for us by God in His very own word! God's thoughts are revealed through Scripture using three essential principles.

Principle 1: Let the Bible interpret itself. Only God can explain what He means.

God's thoughts are manifested by stringing together Scriptures from various books throughout the Bible. Isaiah 28:9-10 gives us the first key to effective Bible study: "Whom will He teach knowledge? And whom will He make to understand the message? Those just weaned from milk? Those just drawn from the breasts? For precept must be upon precept, precept upon precept, line upon line, line upon line, here a little, there a little." Individual subjects are strands woven into the Bible, forming a tapestry that allows us to see and understand what God is accomplishing on earth. These verses in Isaiah 28 are not meant to make us feel inadequate to study God's word, even if we are "uneducated babes" in the Scriptures. God says in Matthew 11:25, "At that time Jesus answered and said, 'I thank you, Father, Lord of heaven and earth, that You have hidden these things from the wise and prudent and have revealed them to babes.'" Oftentimes education and previous assumptions are a hindrance more than a help. God is predisposed to help the common and the humble first, as He says in His well-known statement, "Many who are first will be last, and the last first" (Mark 10:31).

The beautiful concept of God's woven thoughts is eloquently conveyed in Isaiah 55 verses 8-11: "'For My thoughts are not your thoughts, nor are your ways My ways,' says the Lord. 'For as the heavens are higher than the earth, so are My ways higher than your ways, and My thoughts than your thoughts. For as the rain comes down, and the snow from heaven, and do not return there, but water the earth, and make it bring forth and bud, that it may give seed to the sower and bread to the eater, so shall My word be that goes forth from My mouth; it shall not return to Me void, but it shall accomplish what I please, and it shall prosper in the thing for which I sent it.'"

God will succeed in all that He intends to do, and His mind envisions more than mankind could ever imagine. In the Hebrew, the word for His thoughts is *machashebeth* (#4284 Strong 1995), meaning His plan and intentions that He weaves and plaits within His word. Just as physical rain leads to earth's bounty, so His recorded thoughts are for nourishing the minds and hearts of man. His thoughts on many diverse subjects are woven into the Bible from Genesis to Revelation. With His help, we will string together His thoughts on how He intends to deliver the world from its current nightmare. The Bible contains God's thoughts on thousands of subjects. This book will confine itself to several lines of thought to help us get a good idea of how God intends to help us at this pivotal time in history. But just as it is better to teach a man to fish, it is the most helpful to have the spiritual language skills that unlock the deeper thoughts of God.

Principle 2: Physical and spiritual parallels.

Looking into the Bible is much like observing the physical universe. We can take a walk outside and see grass, trees, mountains, lakes, rivers, and the sea. We can look up and see the sun, moon, stars, and clouds. Whether we look up or down, we can do so with greater intensity. We can employ the use of telescopes or microscopes and find the universe to be vastly bigger or smaller than we ever imagined. The universe is full of enormous galaxies composed of tiny subatomic particles. The mind of God both conceived the universe and inspired the Bible. Therefore all of creation has His fingerprints on it. Every aspect of creation reveals something about the mind and thoughts of God.

Only the Bible contains the language of His spoken thoughts. Therefore, only the Bible can be used to peer into His mind with the power of a microscope or a telescope. The Bible holds tiny details as well as grand design. Observation of physical creation combined with the Bible is what makes it possible to understand God's thoughts. It is very, very important to grasp why this is so. As we read and study the Bible, always remember that physical creation parallels a spiritual creation. Physical creation is the mirror image of a realm we cannot see with the naked eye. The Bible constantly refers to both realms, often doing so at the same time in the same Scripture.

The following Scriptures allow us to confidently accept the second principle that the physical realm is a tool to understand the spiritual. Romans 1:20 states: "For since the creation of the world His invisible attributes are clearly seen, being understood by the things that are made, even His eternal power and Godhead" (divine nature or mind). Psalm 19:1-6 states: "The heavens declare the glory of God; and the firmament shows His handiwork. Day unto day utters speech, and night unto night reveals knowledge. There is no speech nor language where their voice is not heard. Their line [sound] has gone out through all the earth, and their words to the end of the world. In them He has set a tabernacle for the sun, which is like a bridegroom coming out of his chamber, and rejoices like a strong man to run its race. Its rising is from one end of heaven, and its circuit to the other end; and there is nothing hidden from its heat." Without physical creation and the meaning it conveys, we could not hope to understand God's thoughts.

Principle 3: Former and latter fulfillment of prophecy.

A third key principle for understanding the Bible is that most of the prophecies have former and latter fulfillments. In other words, prophecies are often dual in nature. The former or early fulfillment took place from Christ's death looking backwards in history. The latter or second fulfillment takes place from Christ's death looking forward. Without this critical understanding, it is easy to become confused. Many rabbis are convinced that all of the prophecies of the Old Testament have been fulfilled with the exception of the coming Messiah. This leads to a disregard of the New Testament.

Most New Testament prophecy is incomprehensible without the former fulfillment of the Old Testament. This is akin to trying to understand the present and see into the future without a knowledge of history. We need the information contained in the Old *and* New Testaments for God's thoughts to make sense.

In both the Old Testament and New Testament, the Bible speaks of former (early) rain and latter rain. James 5 verse 7: "Therefore be patient, brethren, until the coming of the Lord. See how the farmer waits for the precious fruit of the earth, waiting patiently for it until it receives the early and latter rain." From the Old Testament we will read Hosea 6 verse 3: "Let us know, let us pursue the knowledge of the Lord. His going forth is established as the morning; He will come to us like the rain, like the latter and former rain to the earth." God's thoughts are a type of rain that falls upon the earth. Isaiah 55 verses 10-11: "'For as the rain comes down, and the snow from heaven, and do not return there, but water the earth, and make it bring forth and bud, that it may give seed to the sower and bread to the eater, so shall My word be that goes forth from My mouth; it shall not return to Me void, but it shall accomplish what I please, and it shall prosper in the thing for which I sent it.'" We need only to look at the overall Bible to see that it comes in two halves, the Old Testament from Genesis to Christ, and the New Testament from Christ to the Book of Revelation. The Old Testament forms early or first rain showers, and the New Testament forms the latter rain showers. We can also see that when we study God's word, it is important to get it right. We need to hear what God says in His rain. "Former rain" derives from the Hebrew word *mowreh* (#4175 Strong 1995) and can be thought of as the early teaching rain. "Latter rain" is "the spring rain…figuratively eloquence" (#4456 Strong 1995).

Old Testament prophecies really did apply to ancient Israel and have been fulfilled. However, many of those prophecies were also history written in advance for those who would eventually follow Christ. In addition, New Testament prophecies work in concert with Old Testament prophecies with the express purpose of being a help to those alive at the end of the age. I Corinthians 10:1-5 helps us understand this while utilizing both Principles 1 and 2: "Moreover, brethren, I do not want you to be unaware that all our fathers were under the cloud, all passed through the sea, all were baptized into Moses in the cloud and in the sea, all ate the same spiritual food, and all drank the same spiritual drink. For they drank of that spiritual Rock that followed them, and that Rock was Christ. But with most of them God was not well pleased, for their bodies were scattered in the wilderness." After detailing several calamities that befell ancient Israel, verses 11 and 12 go on to say, "Now all these things happened to them as examples, and they were written for our admonition, upon whom the ends of the ages have come. Therefore let him who thinks he stands take heed lest he fall."

Underlying all good Bible study is God's help. We need Him to guide us to use His principles and His word correctly.

The best way to study the Bible is with humility, realizing how helpless and small we are compared to God. God gives grace to the humble (I Peter 5:5). The deep mysteries of the Bible are understood by the Holy Spirit, which is the mind power of Jesus Christ, working within our natural mind. That Spirit guides us into all truth by opening our minds to the truth contained in the Bible (John 16:13-15). It is imperative to realize that there is no more prophecy to be written after the Book of Revelation (Revelation 22:18-19). There is no need for more prophecy, but rather a great need to know more about the prophetic words already in the pages of the Bible. The amount of knowledge contained in its pages is probably infinite. God promises to reveal enough of His thoughts in the latter days to keep us busy digesting those thoughts. A humble, teachable mind allowing His Spirit to work with it is the only prerequisite. After reading the following texts, we will embark on our journey into the mind of God through the portal of His word, letting Him explain His own thoughts through His own words.

I Corinthians 2 verses 9-16: "But as it is written: 'Eye has not seen nor ear heard, nor have entered into the heart of man the things which God has prepared for those who love Him.' [quoting Isaiah 64:4] But God has revealed them to us through His Spirit. For the Spirit searches all things, yes, the deep things of God. For what man knows the things of a man except the spirit of the man which is in him? [speaking of human reasoning power] Even so no one knows the things of God except the Spirit of God. Now we have received, not the spirit of the world, but the Spirit who is from God, that we might know the things that have been freely given to us by God. These things we also speak, not in the words which man's wisdom teaches but which the Holy Spirit teaches, comparing spiritual things with spiritual. But the natural man does not receive the things of the Spirit of God, for they are foolishness to him; nor can he know them, because they are spiritually discerned. But he who is spiritual judges all things, yet he himself is rightly judged by no one. For 'who has known the mind of the Lord that he may instruct

Him?' [quoting Isaiah 40:13] But we have the mind of Christ."

Until the last days, the mind of Christ was shared by God with just a few. However, we have entered that time Scripture calls the latter days, which makes Peter's inspired words in Acts 2:17-18 very exciting and encouraging to the whole world: "And it shall come to pass in the last days, says God, that I will pour out My Spirit on all flesh; your sons and daughters shall prophesy, your young men shall see visions, your old men shall dream dreams. And on My menservants and on My maidservants I will pour out My Spirit in those days; and they shall prophesy." From the time Peter uttered those words, quoting the Old Testament prophet Joel, understanding has been slowly building and spreading until it will explode across the earth in the last days. The word "prophesy" in these verses comes from the Greek *propheteuo* (#4395 Strong 1995), meaning to be able to understand and speak about God's word by His inspiration. By no means is it implying that people are free to write more Scripture or prophecy. The foundational teachings have all been recorded for us at the hands of the prophets of the Old Testament and the apostles of the New Testament (Ephesians 2:19-20, Luke 11:49). There is no need to feel slighted by this, as it is as great a miracle to understand what is written in the Bible as it is to have actually penned the words. Both require God's inspiration and direction. Therefore all of us need to pray humbly for inspiration asking God to reveal His thoughts to us through His word, creation, prophetic dual fulfillments, and an understanding of how the physical and spiritual realms work.

As we saw, defining the term "Revelation" is important in order to begin debunking the doom and gloom scenarios. Revelation comes from the Greek word *apokalupsis* (#602 Strong 1995), which means to unveil or disclose. The discovery of something previously unknown is exciting and interesting. However, God does not inspire Scripture just to be exciting and interesting. There is a purpose behind it all (II Timothy 3:16).

The ultimate purpose of the Book of Revelation is in harmony with the whole Bible. God promises every human being a chance to overcome and help defeat evil. Romans 12:21 tells us: "Do not be overcome by evil, but overcome evil with good." We are told in Revelation 21:7 that: "He who overcomes shall inherit all things, and

I will be His God and he shall be My son." "Overcome" is derived from the Greek *nikao*, meaning "to subdue" (#3528 Strong 1995). Every human being has struggled with the forces of evil in his life. Both history and the current world stage are littered with human failure. Weapons of mass destruction, natural disaster, famine, and disease make the future seem hopeless. However, do not hold that view, because the book of Revelation reveals how God, working with humanity, will defeat evil and deliver us from it.

Those who read the Book of Revelation and envision cataclysm and catastrophe are not hearing the words as God breathed them. They do not hear God's voice. Eight times the book of Revelation uses the phrase, "he who has an ear, let him hear what the Spirit says to the churches." Hearing the voice of God through His breathed-out words of Scripture is a miracle. Just as the physical ear is something we are born with and then train and develop over time, so is spiritual hearing. It is given by God at His discretion but then becomes the responsibility of the recipient to develop and heed. James 1:22 says, "But be doers of the word, and not hearers only…"

We live in a time when it is physically possible to hear God's word more than ever before. It has never been so easy for the masses to possess a copy of the word of God. Thanks to the efforts and sacrifices of many dedicated people, God's word has now been translated into every major language on earth, as well as almost every minor language and dialect. Political and ideological advances now make it possible for almost anyone to own a Bible. Spiritual ability to hear the word of God is a separate matter that God controls. When the ability to hear is present within a person, the possibility to make enlightened choices follows. We are on the threshold of a truly unique time in history – a time when any and all can possess the ability to hear God's voice.

4
The History of Spiritual Hearing

The subject of hearing the voice of God is a fascinating one. The history of hearing God speak can be divided into three distinct periods of time or epochs: from the Garden of Eden until Moses and Mount Sinai, from Mount Sinai until Christ, and from Christ until the present. Each epoch covers approximately two thousand years. During the first epoch, God's words had not been written yet. The only way to hear His thoughts was for Him or one of His angel representatives to communicate directly with a person, who then passed on the message as oral history. Those God chose to speak with are those we call the patriarchs: Enoch, Noah, Abraham, Jacob, etc. They were the only ones privileged to hear God.

The second epoch was from Moses until Christ. This is the period in which God's words were recorded on scrolls that later became the books of the Old Testament. God inspired the highlights of history to be recorded, so they are both accurate and authentic. Moses, under inspiration, wrote the history and prophecy of the first epoch when he wrote the first five books of the Bible, called the Pentateuch: Genesis, Exodus, Leviticus, Numbers, and Deuteronomy.

The first epoch transitioned into the second when Moses heard God's voice at the burning bush in Exodus 3. This humble man was commissioned to lead ancient Israel out of its bondage in Egypt. From this point forward, God's thoughts were to be conveyed to a whole nation, not just to one patriarch at a time. At the time of Moses, it is estimated that the descendants of the patriarchs had grown to about 3.5 million people, divided into the twelve tribes of Israel. After being set free from Egypt, this nation made an agreement with God to be His own special people at a mountain called Sinai. The rest of the world was oblivious to what occurred at Mount Sinai, but the course of history was altered in a profound way. Moses recorded how an entire nation heard God's voice in Exodus 19 and 20. The following verses give us a feel for what it must have been like. Exodus 19 verses 4-8: "'You have seen what I did to the Egyptians, and how I bore you on eagles' wings and brought you to Myself. Now therefore, if you will indeed obey My voice and keep My covenant, then you shall be a special treasure to Me above all people; for all the earth is Mine. And you shall be to Me a kingdom of priests and a holy nation. These are the words you shall speak to the children of Israel.' So Moses came and called the elders of the people, and laid before them all these words which the Lord commanded him. Then all the people answered together and said, 'All that the Lord has spoken we will do.'"

Three days later the agreement was ratified and the law given. Verses 16-21: "Then it came to pass on the third day, in the morning, that there were thunderings and lightnings, and a thick cloud on the mountain; and the sound of the trumpet was very loud, so that all the people who were in the camp trembled. And Moses brought the people out of the camp to meet with God, and they stood at the foot of the mountain. Now Mount Sinai was completely in smoke, because the Lord descended upon it in fire. Its smoke ascended like the smoke of a furnace, and the whole mountain quaked greatly. And when the blast of the trumpet sounded long and became louder and louder, Moses spoke, and God answered him by voice. Then the Lord came down upon Mount Sinai, on the top of the mountain. And the Lord called Moses to the top of the mountain, and Moses went up. And the Lord said to Moses, 'Go down and warn the people, lest they break through to gaze at the Lord, and many of them perish.'" Exodus 20 verses 18-19: "Now all the people witnessed the thunderings, the lightning flashes, the sound of the trumpet, and the mountain smoking; and when the people saw it, they trembled and stood afar off. Then they said to Moses, 'You speak with us, and we will hear; but let not God speak with us, lest we die.'"

From that day forward for over 1500 years, God spoke to the people through the prophets. During that epoch, many achievements set the stage for the final epoch. Four of which to take note are: 1. The entire Old Testament was recorded at the hand of the prophets. 2. The direct lineage continued that would result in the birth of Christ. 3. The Ten Commandments and accompanying statutes were given so the people would have a way to recognize sin and disobedience. 4. A system of sacrifices was given in order to have sins and offenses forgiven.

The work and experiences of ancient Israel, particularly the tribe of Judah, bring us to the final epoch before the deliverance of mankind. The third epoch of time that the Bible calls the latter days began with John the Baptist's life. He marked the transition from the second to the third epoch. The world once again has been oblivious to what has occurred in the last two thousand years, but that is about to change. This final epoch began with only a few who had ears to hear. That tiny number was comprised of John the Baptist, Christ's twelve disciples, and a small group of believers. Christ specifically limited the ability to hear, as is made clear in Matthew 13:10-17. Most people assume that Christ often spoke in parables in order to make things clearer. In actuality, parables were more like riddles that could only be unlocked with the right kind of hearing.

This becomes obvious when we read the parable of the sower in Matthew 13:3-9 and the exchange between Christ and the disciples which followed: "Then He spoke many things to them in parables, saying: 'Behold, a sower went out to sow. And as he sowed, some seed fell by the wayside; and the birds came and devoured them. Some fell on stony places, where they did not have much earth; and they immediately sprang up because they had no depth of earth. But when the sun was up they were scorched, and because they had no root they withered away. And some fell among thorns, and the thorns sprang up and choked them. But others fell on good ground and yielded a crop: some a hundredfold, some sixty, some thirty. He who has ears to hear, let him hear!'" Here is the exchange that followed. "And the disciples came and said to Him, 'Why do you speak to them in parables?' He answered and said to them, 'Because it has been given to you to know the mysteries of the kingdom of heaven, but to them it has not been given. For whoever has, to him more will be given, and he will have abundance; but whoever does not have, even what he has will be taken away from him. Therefore I speak to them in parables, because seeing they do not see, and hearing they do not hear, nor do they understand. And in them the prophecy of Isaiah is fulfilled, which says, "Hearing you will hear and not understand, and seeing you will see and not perceive; for the hearts of this people have grown dull. Their ears are hard of hearing, and their eyes they have closed""" (Isaiah 6:9-10). Verses

16-17 conclude, "But blessed are your eyes for they see, and your ears for they hear; for assuredly, I say to you that many prophets and righteous men desired to see what you see, and did not see it, and to hear what you hear, and did not hear it." At the very beginning, Christ told us that this hearing is something we are given. It is therefore supernatural, something beyond normal physical hearing.

Christ was not being unfair, but rather careful and kind. To hear and understand the truth comes with responsibility and sacrifice. Things are being done in an order that will ensure that all will be well in the end for the maximum number of people. For those who are able to see and hear first, it is indeed a very difficult course. With the passing of time it is getting easier and easier.

Using the principles of former and latter fulfillment, just think for a moment about all that ancient Israel, and specifically the Jewish people, endured. Because they heard the voice of God first, they have suffered the most for the longest period of time. The world indeed owes them a huge debt of gratitude, for without them we would not have the Old Testament Scriptures, Jesus Christ the Messiah, or His disciples who penned the New Testament. They were all Jewish. The early Church until Paul was one hundred percent Jewish, and through them the foundation was built that all who followed might have firm ground to stand on. Ancient Israel, including Judah, was the first nation to have a special relationship with God.

Abraham, the father of the Israelite people, and the spiritual father of all the faithful in Christ (Hebrews 11), was given a promise by God in Genesis 22:10-18 for being willing to offer up his only son Isaac as a sacrifice. This act made the former and latter fulfillments as well as the duality principles apply to God the Father offering up His only Son, thus fulfilling prophecy. "By myself I have sworn, says the Lord, because you have done this thing, and have not withheld your son, your only son – blessing I will bless you, and multiplying I will multiply your descendants as the stars of the heaven and as the sand which is on the seashore; and your descendants shall possess the gate of their enemies. In your seed all the nations of the earth shall be blessed, because you have obeyed My voice." (Genesis 22:16-18) The Apocalypse reveals the mysterious path God chose to take on the way to worldwide deliverance and the time just ahead when all mankind will hear God's voice.

5

The Four Horsemen of the Apocalypse

Revelation chapter 6 opens with the four horsemen of the Apocalypse riding across the earth's surface, dispensing death, destruction, and suffering. Descriptions of each horse and rider are rolled up in a scroll under separate seals. This mysterious scroll exists in heaven and had been sealed for an unidentified length of time. No man had been found worthy to open it to reveal its contents until Jesus Christ lived a perfect life, died, and was resurrected. Revelation 5:1-5 explains how only Christ could take the scroll from the hand of God the Father and reveal its contents: "And I saw in the right hand of Him who sat on the throne a scroll written inside and on the back, sealed with seven seals. Then I saw a strong angel proclaiming with a loud voice, 'Who is worthy to open the scroll and to loose its seals?' And no one in heaven or on the earth or under the earth was able to open the scroll, or to look at it. But one of the elders said to me, 'Do not weep. Behold, the Lion of the tribe of Judah, the Root of David, has prevailed to open the scroll and to loose its seven seals.'" The Lion of the tribe of Judah, the Root of David, is none other than Jesus Christ, and He selected the apostle John to witness the opening of the scroll and record the contents in a book.

The four horsemen have been riding throughout human history. When John saw the first four seals opened, he was looking both into the past and into the future.

John was given the supernatural power to see beyond the veil which separates the physical and spiritual realms. He was able to see into a place where time as we know it does not exist. It is very important to keep this in mind because the book of Revelation often shifts from past, to present, to future, and back again as it links together cause and effect, history, and prophecy. John is told this in chapter 1 verse 19: "Write the things you have seen, and the things which are, and the things which will take place after this."

The first four seals that were opened revealed to John what

had been happening on earth during the previous four thousand years (six thousand years, from our point of view). John sees four powerful demonic princes, each able to wreak havoc on mankind by using powerful hidden influence. Each horse symbolizes a type of influence.

Under the first seal is a rider on a white horse, symbolizing the lies of false religion and ideologies (Revelation 6:2).

The second rider is on a fiery red horse, granted to take peace from the earth through war, hatred, tyranny, and prejudice.

The third rides a black horse, symbolizing famine.

The fourth and last horse is a pale horse, symbolizing death by all other sources.

These four demonic princes serve under Satan, their ruler and master. Descending in order of rank are at least 200 million other demons (Revelation 9:16). They are arranged in a governmental structure akin to a military dictatorship. Humanity is held prisoner in the iron grip of their influence. These beings bear ultimate responsibility for human misery. All of these beings are organized to exert influence over every geographical and political region on earth, from the largest nations and empires to the smallest principalities and ethnic divides. Ephesians 6:2 explains, "For we do not wrestle against flesh and blood, but against principalities, against powers, against the rulers of the darkness of this age, against spiritual hosts of wickedness in the heavenly places." The "darkness of this age" can also be translated "darkness of this world." "World" comes from the Greek word *aion* (#165 Strong 1995), from which we get eon or age. When the Bible speaks of the end of the world, it is talking about the end of Satan's age, not a destructive end to the physical globe. The end of this age coincides with the end of evil influence.

How Satan Wreaks Havoc
God and His system are diametrically opposed to Satan and his system. In Chapter 3 we covered how God's word was divinely inspired by God's wind or breath. God's word can be properly heard when we have ears to hear. That same word, when heard, enters the mind like seed, which under the right circumstances grows to bear fruit. We covered the parable of the sower, which demonstrates that

God is a spiritual farmer growing crops of good character here on earth. When God formed Adam of the dust (dirt) of the ground, His plan was to make him the start of His garden to spread and fill the whole earth with people, providing the fertile soil to grow and develop untold billions in His image and likeness. Man's body and mind are the soil, and God provides the rain and sun (doctrine and truth). God is a good farmer seeking crops of righteousness, joy, peace, love, and compassion.

Satan is the direct opposite, a being seeking to produce crops that mirror his character filled with lies, deceit, violence, greed, and hatred. His wind or breath is akin to hissing, an evil whispering in the ear. This wind also carries upon it the seeds of evil that land in our minds, sprout, take root, and grow. With his evil wind and seed, he takes peace from the earth. His wind and rain form violent storms upon humanity. The hissing of Satan and his demons is carried upon the air like a radio or TV broadcast looking for a tuned-in receiver. Hence, Ephesians 2:2 calls him, "…the prince of the power of the air, the spirit who now works in the sons of disobedience."

Evil winds constantly blow back and forth over the earth. Satan's influence causes a host of ills leading to murder, racism, and other crimes. Satan's hissing is most dangerous when it "inspires" a willing recipient to produce destructive ideologies that move the masses in great waves of hatred and violence. The Twentieth Century saw many examples of this under the tyranny of such men as Adolf Hitler, Joseph Stalin, and Mao Tse-Tung. Dangerous ideology sprouting in the minds of these men eventually led to the death of 150 million people and accompanying human suffering which is incalculable. Satan indeed plants noxious weeds. The four horsemen certainly drive mankind toward war, directly resulting in death and destruction, but the resulting after effects may go on for years, even generations. Famine, disease, pestilence, poverty, and oppression are difficult shackles to remove.

Jesus Christ talked about mankind as the soil of His farm field in the parable of the sower in Matthew 13 verses 24-30: "Another parable He put forth to them, saying: 'The kingdom of heaven is like a man who sowed good seed in his field; but while men slept, his enemy came and sowed tares among the wheat and went his way. But when the grain had sprouted and produced a crop, then the tares also appeared. So the servants of the owner came and said to him, "Sir, did you not sow good seed in your field? How then does it have tares?" He said to them, "An enemy has done this." The servants said to him, "Do you want us then to go and gather them up?" But he said, "No, lest while you gather up the tares you also uproot the wheat with them. Let both grow together until the harvest, and at the time of harvest I will say to the reapers, 'First gather together the tares and bind them in bundles to burn them, but gather the wheat into my barn.'"''" Christ explained the parable a little later when He was alone with His disciples as recorded in verses 37-40: "He answered and said to them: 'He who sows the good seed is the Son of Man. The field is the world, the good seeds are the sons of the kingdom, but the tares are the sons of the wicked one. The enemy who sowed them is the devil, the harvest is the end of the age, and the reapers are the angels. Therefore as the tares are gathered and burned in the fire, so it will be at the end of this age.'" As we delve into the Book of Revelation, it will become clear that God intends for the earth to bear fruit with incredible abundance at the end of the age.

In order to understand how barren the earth has been up to this point in time, we need to look at the galloping horse of famine from a different perspective. Physical emaciation has its spiritual and intellectual counterpart in the form of ignorance. A complete and balanced knowledge is not attainable through the scientific method alone. It must have God's truth as its foundation and main pillars. Good scientific facts always corroborate the real mind behind the physics and laws of the universe which is the mind of God. The towering intellects of people like Newton, Einstein, and Sagan are capable of scientific discovery in physics, astronomy, and mathematics. However, all scientific theories, equations, and discoveries can do nothing to shed light on the whys and wherefores of creation. Only God can convey what, why, and for what purpose. God communicates through His word, the Bible. Scientific discoveries, when understood in the proper context of God's purposes, confirm God's word.

Unfortunately, Satan's ill winds have often inspired dogmatic adherence to incorrect doctrines and beliefs wrested out of context from the Bible. Fanatical observance to false dogmas has often given rise to cruel and inhumane behavior. Throughout history, dogmatism has been followed by the thundering hooves of war, famine, and death. Sadly, this has caused many of our greatest minds to disregard the Bible as a valuable source of knowledge, thus disconnecting God's communication to mankind from the corroboration of scientific discovery. When science brushes aside God's word as intellectually inferior, they close the only portal God gave us to enter His mind and thoughts. Satan has kept mankind in ignorance of God through false doctrines and beliefs, unsound ideology, and science disconnected from His word. By this combination Satan has held the earth in his iron grip, hoping to lead mankind toward annihilation which unfettered science makes possible. The removal of Satan's influence is the key to peace on earth, and it is God's truth that will set us free (John 8:32) and protect us from ignorantly and helplessly falling victim to Satan's devices. The Book of Revelation explains the mystery of how this earthly garden can be transformed from a vale of tears to a fruitful paradise by stopping the four horsemen from trampling it.

6

The Purpose of Light - The Essence of Time

"In the beginning God created the heavens and the earth. The earth was without form, and void; and darkness was on the face of the deep. And the Spirit of God was hovering over the face of the waters. Then God said, 'Let there be light'; and there was light" (Genesis 1:1-3). The decision to shed light on the earth did more than change the course of history. It created the specific road that history would follow. God's plan and strategy was devised to eventually eliminate evil while at the same time to replace the perpetrators of evil with beings made in His image and likeness. Unfortunately, this transcendent purpose is often overshadowed or totally lost in the age-old arguments and speculation about the time frame and accuracy of the Genesis creation.

The genealogical records in the Bible prove beyond a doubt that the Genesis story took place six thousand years ago. Irrefutable scientific discoveries prove that the earth and sun are thirteen to fifteen billion years old. Careful analysis demonstrates that both views are correct, with science actually confirming God's word, not refuting it.

Genesis is the book of beginnings, and it alludes to more than one beginning. The Bible opens with God's Spirit hovering over an earth without form and void: an earth already in existence! Therefore the Book of Genesis is not detailing the events of the original creation of the universe, but rather a new beginning for earth itself. Scripture does not say how much time elapsed between the beginning mentioned in verse 1 and God's Spirit hovering over the earth. Science has determined it is probably on the order of thirteen to fifteen billion years. Fossil records clearly reveal that life has existed on earth for hundreds of millions of years. So what exactly happened six thousand years ago? Answers lie in the meaning of the ancient Hebrew words that comprise verse 2. Let's reread that Scripture and examine its key words.

"The earth was without form, and void; and darkness was on the face of the deep. And the Spirit of God was hovering over the face of the waters."

"Form" is *tohuw*: "to lie waste; a desolation (of surface), i.e. desert; figuratively a worthless thing" (#8414 Strong 1995).

"Void" is *bohuw*: (#922 Strong 1995) a vacuum or indistinguishable ruin.

"Hovering" is *rachaph*: "to brood" (#7363 Strong 1995).

"Darkness" is *choshek*: "misery, destruction, death, ignorance, sorrow, wickedness" (#2822 Strong 1995).

"Waters" is *mayim*: "water, figuratively juice; by euphemism urine, semen," (#4325 Strong 1995), waste water.

Now, utilizing the fuller depth of meaning in Hebrew, we could render verse 2 this way: The Spirit of God was brooding in thought over what to do about the desolation and ruin that had taken place on earth. Looking across its surface, God saw misery, destruction, death, ignorance, sorrow, and wickedness. The fruit of the earth was to Him the equivalent of waste water, suitable for no good purpose.

What God proposed to do about the evil was to let His light shine through the darkness, pushing it aside, calling the darkness Night and His light Day. He then separated the waste water from firm ground, upon which He would have a garden called Eden. For the rest of what has been called creation week, He attached meaning and significance to physical things, some animate and some inanimate. Throughout the rest of the Bible, one of His purposes would be to define the significance of each in terms that would reveal His plans and purposes. Light itself would be the prime instrument of His will to push back evil darkness. Therefore light is His truth, knowledge, and wisdom, as opposed to Satan's lies and deceit.

Verse 16 reveals that God's light would be brought to the earth in three primary ways. "Then God made two great lights: the greater light to rule the day, and the lesser light to rule the night. He made the stars also [to rule the night]." To rule means exactly that – to govern over as a ruler over a realm. Once again we see that creation was already here in the form of the sun, moon, and stars. But verses 14 and 15 show us God was now going to attach spiritual meaning and significance to what we see when we look up into the heavens. The meaning would be used by Him to form language by which He would convey His thoughts to humanity, as we discussed in Chapter 3.

Let's read verses 14 and 15, then analyze them: "Then God said, 'Let there be lights in the firmament of the heavens to divide the day from the night; and let them be for signs and seasons and for days and years.'" The sun or moon can be used for the basis for a calendar. Most cultures on earth today use the 365.25 day solar year. There are a few who use the 354.37 day lunar year. Either calendar can be used for taking note of physical time in the form of days, weeks, months, and years. Each year is easily divided into seasons which can be matched to natural cycles on earth. For example, spring is for planting and new life; summer for growth; fall for harvest; and winter as a dead or dormant season. Each seasonal cycle is directly driven by the position of the sun in relation to the earth and moon.

Amazingly, there is a third calendar revealed in verses 14-15. Where the first two calendars merely keep track of physical time, this one keeps track of prophetic time. On this calendar, physical and spiritual reality meet together at designated times. Without a working knowledge of prophetic time, much of the Bible remains locked up in mystery and is prone to be wildly misinterpreted. In Chapter 9 we will have a much more detailed discussion of prophetic time. It is necessary to establish more groundwork first. For now we will determine what God means by signs and seasons in the Hebrew, using Strong's Concordance (1995 edition).

"Signs" is *owth*: (#226 Strong 1995) signals to appear literally or figuratively as a flag, beacon, monument, omen, prodigy, and evidence like a miracle or signifying mark.

"Seasons" is *mowed*: "an appointment, i.e. a fixed time or season; specifically a festival; conventionally a year; by implication an assembly (as convened for a definite purpose); technically the congregation; by extension the place of meeting" (#4150 Strong 1995), as a predetermined signal.

In other words, the sun and the moon together provide information to be used as evidence to designate predetermined times and seasons. Within those times and seasons there are scheduled appointments for congregational assembly for specific purposes.

This is another type of calendar, keeping track of predetermined assemblies to occur on a schedule of events that God has prophesied will occur. God designated these events to occur during the four seasons needed to turn the earth into a productive garden.

Every nation, culture, and religion takes annual note of days with historical and religious significance to them, i.e. Independence Day, Armistice Day, Christmas, New Year's Day, etc. Most such noted days look backward in time. In Genesis, God said He would use the sun and moon to look forward in time towards significant events He has predetermined. The ultimate purpose of these events is to defeat evil and liberate mankind from all forms of tyranny and oppression.

The Bible as One Unified Book

Before continuing with Genesis, it is crucial to realize that the Bible is one unified book. Though it is broken down into sixty-six separate books, each complete in its own right, all of these books taken together form a panoramic view of the past, present, and future. Yet each book also contained valuable information useful to the specific people to whom it was given at the time it was written. Forty-four authors wrote over a period of fifteen centuries, each picking up where the other left off and each providing crucial segments that fit perfectly in the continuum. This attests to the vastness and superiority of the mind of God. This means, however, that to plumb the depth of His mind on a given matter we must search the whole Bible to understand the subject in question.

So it is with the spiritual meaning attached to the sun, moon, and stars we see above. In brief, the sun represents Jesus Christ, the moon represents God's people, and the stars represent angels. Malachi 4:2 calls Christ the Sun of Righteousness. John 1:1-8 calls Christ the Light of the world. John 9:4 says that while Christ walked the earth, it was day. Just as the physical moon above reflects the light of the sun, so God's people are to reflect Christ's light. Hence, Matthew 5:14-16 calls Christ's followers "the light of the world." Revelation 1:20 shows that stars represent angels. This understanding alone opens up many obscure biblical passages and is the first step in telling prophetic time. The Bible is replete with references to prophetic times and seasons, days and years, and as we touch on them in this book, our knowledge will build so we will be able to tell prophetic time. More importantly, we will be able to participate in some of the events that God predetermined before time itself existed.

7

Working in the Garden

The creative process in Genesis chapters 1 and 2 was not simply to bring the earth into initial existence, as we have already noted. God wanted to refurbish or renew what was already on earth and make it conducive to His overall purpose. The words "create" and "created" used throughout the Old Testament are translated from the Hebrew word *bara*. The word *bara* can be used in the absolute sense to create, but in a qualified sense it means "to cut down (a wood), select, feed (as formative processes)" (#1254 Strong 1995). In a sense, it is undoing the damage that had been done to creation, forming it into something useful to Him. God will restore the peace and perfection that existed before Lucifer became evil.

God names things what they are in terms of likeness or character. Before God's greatest archangel had the name Satan, which means "an opponent… the arch-enemy of good… adversary" (#7854 Strong 1995), he had the name Lucifer. "Lucifer" means to be bright like the morning star, to shine brightly, to be clear. Lucifer, as the top angel, was the chief light-bringer in the universe. He was in charge of handling God's directives in the hierarchy of angelic beings. Let's read how his character took an evil turn in the following two sets of Scriptures.

Isaiah 14 verses 12-15: "How you are fallen from heaven, O Lucifer, son of the morning! How you are cut down to the ground, you who weakened the nations! For you have said in your heart: 'I will ascend into heaven, I will exalt my throne above the stars of God; I will also sit on the mount of the congregation on the farthest sides of the north; I will ascend above the heights of the clouds, I will be like the Most High.' Yet you shall be brought down to Sheol, to the lowest depths of the Pit." Pride is what led to Lucifer's fall, causing him to become the arch-enemy of God. Verse 4 calls him the king of Babylon, which is the name of his spiritual realm. The physical empire of Babylon of ancient times was merely a reflection of his character, deceived and led by the ill wind of his influence.

Ezekiel 28:12-17 compares Satan to the king of ancient Tyre and reveals more about his character and previous position in heaven: "Son of man, take up a lamentation for the king of Tyre, and say to him, 'Thus says the Lord God: "You were the seal of perfection, full of wisdom and perfect in beauty. You were in Eden, the garden of God; every precious stone was your covering: the sardius, topaz, and diamond, beryl, onyx, and jasper, sapphire, turquoise, and emerald with gold. The workmanship of your timbrels and pipes was prepared for you on the day you were created. You were the anointed cherub who covers; I established you; you were on the holy mountain of God; you walked back and forth in the midst of fiery stones. You were perfect in your ways from the day you were created, till iniquity was found in you. By the abundance of your trading you became filled with violence within, and you sinned; therefore I cast you as a profane thing out of the mountain of God; and I destroyed you, O covering cherub, from the midst of the fiery stones. Your heart was lifted up because of your beauty; you corrupted your wisdom for the sake of your splendor; I cast you to the ground…"'"

Satan's wicked character forced God to destroy his position at God's throne and cast him out of heaven, limiting his influence to the earth. Cast out along with him were one-third of the angels. Verse 13 of Ezekiel 28 reminds us that Satan was present in the Garden of Eden, so let's go back to Genesis and see what happened there.

Turning to Genesis 1:26-27 finds us at the apex of creation week: "Then God said, 'Let Us make man in Our image, according to Our likeness…So God created man in His own image; in the image of God He created him; male and female He created them." God here speaks of Himself using the Hebrew word *elohiym* (#430 Strong 1995), a uniplural noun like the word family. That is what the God-head is: a family comprised of a Father and a Creator who would eventually become His Son, Jesus Christ. God's ultimate purpose that transcends all others is to increase the size of His family. That is why the New Testament often refers to the followers of Christ as sons of God and brethren (brothers) of Christ. The biggest obstacle to both God and man is, of course, Satan. The success of God's plan will be Satan's ultimate doom. Isaiah 14 and Ezekiel 28 make that clear.

Satan was cast down to the ground only to find that his mortal enemy had become the very dust of the ground, wave after wave of human beings rising up out of the earth that he must defeat. Satan's mission was to make sure God's earthly garden would never produce a single pure human fruit. In the following few Scriptures, it becomes very clear what shape the war between good and evil would take and the outcome God predicts: "And the Lord God formed man of the dust of the ground, and breathed into his nostrils the breath of life; and man became a living being. The Lord God planted a garden eastward in Eden, and there He put the man whom He had formed. And out of the ground the Lord God made every tree grow that is pleasant to the sight and good for food. The tree of life was also in the midst of the garden, and the tree of the knowledge of good and evil…Then the Lord God took the man and put him in the garden of Eden to tend and keep it. And the Lord God commanded the man, saying, 'Of every tree of the garden you may freely eat; but of the tree of the knowledge of good and evil you shall not eat, for in the day that you eat of it you shall surely die.' And the Lord God said, 'It is not good that man should be alone; I will make him a helper comparable to him'…And the Lord God caused a deep sleep to fall on Adam, and he slept; and He took one of his ribs, and closed up the flesh in its place. Then the rib which the Lord God had taken from man He made into a woman, and He brought her to the man. And Adam said: 'This is now bone of my bones and flesh of my flesh; she shall be called Woman, because she was taken out of Man'" (Genesis 2:7-9, 15-18, 21-23).

From the dust of the ground, God made Adam and Eve to work in the garden. It is simplistic to think that their purpose was to raise physical crops. They were created to produce character like God and offspring to do the same. Innocent obedience to God would have protected them from the infectious broadcast of Satan's attitudes. Genesis chapter 3 relates how the cunning serpent got his attitudes into the minds of Adam and Eve by deceitfully appealing to human curiosity. From that point forward, the dust of the ground in God's garden became a mixture of good and evil, good fruit along with choking weeds in the form of sin. Lust of the eyes, lust of the flesh, and the pride of life took deep root, sprouted, and spread seed through the entire human race. Eve had been tricked, and Adam followed along, but God would not be denied the production of good fruit from His earthly garden. It would simply take a little longer, for now it became war between the dust of the ground and Satan. Satan's curse would fit his crime. For instilling evil into humanity, he would have to instill it into every single human being to follow. To fail even one time would eventually bring about his utter defeat.

Satan brought the curse of death on humanity and a curse on himself and his realm. God determined to reverse the curse on man while holding Satan accountable. The battle lines were drawn by God in Genesis 3 verses 13-19: "And the Lord God said to the woman, 'What is this you have done?' The woman said, 'The serpent deceived me, and I ate.' So the Lord God said to the serpent: 'Because you have done this, you are cursed more than all cattle, and more than every beast of the field; on your belly you shall go, and you shall eat dust all the days of your life. And I will put enmity between you and the woman, and between your seed and her Seed; He shall bruise your head, and you shall bruise His heel.' To the woman He said: 'I will greatly multiply your sorrow and your conception; in pain you shall bring forth children; your desire shall be for your husband, and he shall rule over you.' Then to Adam He said, 'Because you have heeded the voice of your wife, and have eaten from the tree of which I commanded you, saying, "You shall not eat of it": cursed is the ground for your sake; in toil you shall eat of it all the days of your life. Both thorns and thistles it shall bring forth for you, and you shall eat the herb of the field. In the sweat of your face you shall eat bread till you return to the ground, for out of it you were taken; for dust you are, and to dust you shall return.'"

As difficult as it is to bear and rear children and to work the land for the physical necessities of life, God was talking about something far deeper and more important. God was saying that developing the fruit of good character was going to be very difficult with Satan's influence hindering mankind every step of the way. Wars, famines, pestilence, hatred, division, greed, and intense competition have shackled mankind ever since. However, there is tremendous cause for hope. God has quietly and successfully been working the earth's soil with another Adam and another Woman. I Corinthians 15:20-26, 45-49, and Ephesians 5 convey this clearly.

"But now Christ is risen from the dead, and has become the firstfruits of those who have fallen asleep. For since by man came death, by Man also came the resurrection of the dead. For as in Adam all die, even so in Christ all shall be made alive. But each one in his own order: Christ the firstfruits, afterward those who are Christ's at His coming. Then comes the end, when He delivers the kingdom to God the Father, when He puts an end to all rule and all authority and power. For He must reign till He has put all enemies under His feet. The last enemy that will be destroyed is death" (I Corinthians 15:20-26).

"And so it is written, 'The first man Adam became a living being.' The last Adam became a life-giving spirit. However the spiritual is not first, but the natural, and afterward the spiritual. The first man was of the earth, made of dust; the second Man is the Lord from heaven. As was the man of dust, so also are those who are made of dust; as is the heavenly Man, so also are those who are heavenly. And as we have borne the image of the man of dust, we shall also bear the image of the heavenly Man" (I Corinthians 15:45-49).

Immediately following man's fall, God's failsafe back-up plan went into effect. Soil was prepared for a second garden composed of dust of the ground in the form of human beings. With much difficulty, the seed of Eve would reproduce and grow into an ever-increasing family of man. From that family tree, God chose a lineage that He determined would produce Jesus Christ, destined to become a second Adam. This Adam had the power to defeat Satan, thus eventually setting man free from his demonic influence, ultimately reversing the curse of death. The line of Abraham, Isaac, and Jacob became God's soil of choice for another garden and yet another genesis.

Nothing was left to chance. Jesus Christ Himself worked with Eve through her offspring until such time as He could enter the human race in order to take on Satan personally, setting in motion the falling dominoes leading to the collapse of his evil empire. Try to imagine a spiritual Christ working with physical people as they grew from one man, Abraham, into a nation. They worked together in truly remarkable ways. The parallels to the creation week are astounding. They separated fertile soil from the raging waves of

Satan's sea of influence. They brought light to an earth covered in the darkness of ignorance. This light was in the form of truth revealed to the prophets as commandments, statutes, prophecies, and the record of history. Working together, the nation of Israel was formed into His kingdom, ruled beneath His perfect law. Eventually Christ dwelt with this national incarnation of Eve in a physical temple built by Solomon. To His beloved Eve He provided food, protection, shelter, and even a way to deal with sin through a sacrificial system.

God knew this system was a very important and necessary foundational step of the real genesis He had envisioned for mankind. A physical Eve working with a spiritual Adam was and is crucial but is not the ultimate goal. The ultimate goal is for mankind to be a physical garden capable of providing Christ with a spiritual helpmate for eventual spiritual offspring. We now glimpse the courage and sheer intellectual power of God! This is the awesome plan God devised before time itself began. In effect, that is what Titus 1:1-3 tells us: "Paul, a bondservant of God and an apostle of Jesus Christ, according to the faith of God's elect and the acknowledgement of the truth which accords with godliness, in hope of eternal life which God, who cannot lie, promised *before time began*, but has in due time manifested His word through preaching, which was committed to me according to the commandments of God our Savior" (emphasis added). The blueprints for God's project were drawn up before the big bang! The creation around us, the Bible, and good science all bear testimony to the unseen hand of God at work in all things (Romans 1:20).

A Woman Works in the Garden

The Book of Revelation contains a short passage of Scripture that broad-brushes six thousand years of human history, from Adam and Eve to the present time. It is the story of a woman working in the garden as a helpmate to Jesus Christ, the second Adam. Revelation 12 verses 1-6: "Now a great sign appeared in heaven: a woman clothed with the sun, with the moon under her feet, and on her head a garland of twelve stars. Then being with child, she cried out in labor and in pain to give birth. And another sign appeared in heaven: behold, a great, fiery red dragon having seven heads and ten horns, and seven diadems on his heads. His tail drew a third of the stars of heaven and threw them to the earth. And the dragon stood before the woman who was ready to give birth, to devour her Child as soon as it was born. She bore a male Child who was to rule all nations with a rod of iron. And her Child was caught up to God and His throne. Then the woman fled into the wilderness, where she has a place prepared by God, that they should feed her there one thousand two hundred and sixty days." In these few verses, the apostle John was allowed to see and record for us the main thread line of God's plan over a four thousand year period. We read in Genesis 3 how Eve and her descendants would labor in pain to give birth. Now we see here that the travail of human childbirth is the physical manifestation of a parallel experience taking place in a spiritual sense. Plainly, the descendants of Eve form a woman clothed with truth (the Son's light) standing on the moon (the solid ground which reflects the light of the Son). Her head is surrounded by twelve stars picturing how she is guided with the help of twelve angels. Each angel specifically assists one tribe of the twelve tribes of Israel. After four thousand years of labor pains in the form of various trials, tests, and persecutions, she gave birth to Christ. He was born through the line of Judah, which is one of the twelve tribes. God's archenemy Satan, whose realm is composed of one-third of the angels represented as stars, sought to destroy the Child. Jesus Christ, the second Adam, was and is the single biggest threat to his realm. Satan literally tried to have Christ killed as an infant by influencing King Herod to kill all children near Bethlehem under the age of two (see Matthew 2:13-23). After Satan failed to kill Christ as an infant, he conspired to cause Christ to sin at every turn. According to God's curse, if he did not cause all the living dust of the ground to sin, he himself would face defeat. Of course, as we know, Christ lived a perfect life, thus delivering a mortal wound to Satan's kingdom. Satan is here described as a dragon whose realm is the earth. From the earth, Satan would incite seven successive kingdoms to subjugate the woman and persecute her with the express purpose of defeating God. Each would be influenced by a specific demon ruler symbolized by the diadem or crown. By jumping ahead to Revelation 17:10-11, we can gain insight as to where John found himself in this chronology: "There are also seven kings. Five have fallen, one is, and the other has not yet come. And when he comes he must continue a short time." Keep in mind that we are interested only in kingdoms that directly tried to defeat God by subjugating the people God was working with, in particular the tribe of Judah which was carrying the specific lineage leading to Christ. History and the Bible confirm that the empires that subjugated the woman between Abraham and Christ are: Egypt, Philistia, Babylon, Media/Persia, Greece, and Rome.

The seventh is a revived Holy Roman Empire which was a union of church and state. The Roman Empire was a ruling kingdom at the time of Christ and the apostle John. About four hundred years after Christ the Roman Empire fell, but the church state within it has existed till now. History reveals that the Roman Emperor Constantine sanctioned the state religion and changed doctrine in 325 A.D. at the Council of Nicea. This forced a huge split in Christendom and led to the persecution of the Jews, other Christian sects and denominations, and other faiths (more details in Chapters 12 and 13). The wars, crusades, pogroms, and inquisitions are too numerous to mention in this book. Suffice it to say however, that the "woman" God continued to work with, a small Church, was among those it persecuted. The deceiving power of Satan's hidden realm has influenced all these empires to do the things they have done "in the name of God." It should be noted that the world seems to be awakening to the errors of the past. The real war has never been between people but between God and Satan, as we saw in Ephesians chapter 6. Perhaps we can discuss more of that later, but for now we must return to the point in time that John wrote the Book of Revelation.

The first five empires had come and gone as subjugating powers, and Rome was the ruling power at the time of Christ. John was told that one conqueror was yet to come who, once victorious, would continue but a short time. By reading verse 8 then verse 11 of Revelation 17, we will be able to deduce that Satan is the powerful being behind these attempts to thwart God: "The beast that you saw was, and is not, and will ascend out of the bottomless pit and go to perdition. And these who dwell on the earth will marvel, whose names are not written in the Book of Life from the foundation of the world, when they see the beast that was, and is not, and yet is...

The beast that was, and is not, is himself also the eighth, and is of the seven, and is going to perdition." It is very valuable knowledge to realize Satan is the beast who is and is not. Satan is a very real spirit being who is not physical, yet his power is manifested in the seven kingdoms He used to fight God, over each of which reigns one of his demonic princes. He himself is the eighth power who reigns supreme over all the others.

Corroboration for these successive kingdoms subjugating God's people, as well as the demonic princes who influence and rule over these kingdoms, can be seen in Daniel chapters 2 and 10. These worldly powers and the evil forces behind them are what the woman labored against to give birth to Christ, the second Adam. Let's read portions of these fascinating chapters. Daniel 10:10-14, 18-21 gives us a glimpse of the heavenly warfare that takes place in a realm we cannot see. After Daniel fasted and prayed twenty-one days, an angel was dispatched from heaven to bring him a message: "Suddenly, a hand touched me, which made me tremble on my knees and on the palms of my hands. And he said to me, 'O Daniel, man greatly beloved, understand the words that I speak to you, and stand upright, for I have now been sent to you.' While he was speaking this word to me, I stood trembling. Then he said to me, 'Do not fear, Daniel, for from the first day that you set your heart to understand, and to humble yourself before God, your words were heard; and I have come because of your words. But the prince of the kingdom of Persia withstood me twenty-one days; and behold, Michael, one of the chief princes, came to help me, for I had been left alone there with the kings of Persia. Now I have come to make you understand what will happen to your people in the *latter days*, for the vision refers to many days yet to come'... Then again, the one having the likeness of a man touched me and strengthened me. And he said, 'O man greatly beloved, fear not! Peace be to you; be strong, yes, be strong!' So when he spoke to me I was strengthened, and said, 'Let my Lord speak, for you have strengthened me.' Then he said, 'Do you know why I have come to you? And now I must return to fight with the prince of Persia; and when I have gone forth, indeed the prince of Greece will come. But I will tell you what is noted in the Scripture of Truth. (No one upholds me against these, except Michael, your prince.'"

This angel messenger fought the evil prince over Persia for three weeks before he could reach Daniel. He only succeeded after Michael, the angel over the tribe of Judah (the star over Judah), came to assist him. Notice that the messenger then had to fight his way back through the evil prince over Persia to return home. In verse 20 the messenger tells Daniel that the prince over Persia would soon be replaced by a prince over Greece. This is noteworthy because that is the same order of the physical human empires which subjugated God's people.

Daniel chapter 2 supplies more information regarding the chronology of empires that Satan used to fight God. You may want to read this interesting chapter in its entirety, but here we will quote enough to prove our point. Daniel 2:1: "Now in the second year of Nebuchadnezzar's reign, Nebuchadnezzar had dreams; and his spirit was so troubled that his sleep left him." Nebuchadnezzar gave his magicians, astrologers, and sorcerers the opportunity to tell him what his dream was and to reveal its meaning. Eventually the Jewish captive, Daniel, was also given the opportunity. After humbling himself in prayer to God, Daniel was given both the dream and its interpretation. We will pick up the story in verse 28 as Daniel is speaking to Nebuchadnezzar:

"But there is a God in heaven who reveals secrets, and He has made known to king Nebuchadnezzar what will be in the *latter days*. Your dream, and the visions of your head upon your bed, were these: As for you, O king, thoughts came to your mind while on your bed, about what would come to pass after this; and He who reveals secrets has made known to you what will be. But as for me, this secret has not been revealed to me because I have more wisdom than anyone living, but for our sakes who make known the interpretation to the king, and that you may know the thoughts of your heart. You, O king, were watching; and behold, a great image! This great image, whose splendor was excellent, stood before you; and its form was awesome. This image's head was of fine gold, its chest and arms of silver, its belly and thighs of bronze, its legs of iron, its feet partly of iron and partly of clay. You watched while a stone was cut out without hands, which struck the image on its feet of iron and clay, and broke them in pieces. Then the iron, the clay, the bronze, the silver, and the gold were crushed together, and became like chaff from the summer threshing floors; the wind carried them away so that no trace of them was found. And the stone that struck the image became a great mountain and filled the whole earth. This is the dream. Now we will tell the interpretation of it before the king.

"You, O king, are a king of kings. For the God of heaven has given you a kingdom, power, strength, and glory; and wherever the children of men dwell, or the beasts of the field and the birds of the heaven, He has given them into your hand, and has made you ruler over them all - you are this head of gold. But after you shall arise another kingdom inferior to yours; then another, a third kingdom of bronze, which shall rule over all the earth. And the fourth kingdom shall be as strong as iron, inasmuch as iron breaks in pieces and shatters everything; and like iron that crushes, that kingdom will break in pieces and crush all the others. Whereas you saw the feet and toes, partly of potter's clay and partly of iron, the kingdom shall be divided; yet the strength of the iron shall be in it, just as you saw the iron mixed with ceramic clay. And as the toes of the feet were partly of iron and partly of clay, so the kingdom will be partly strong and partly fragile. As you saw iron mixed with ceramic clay, they will mingle with the seed of men; but they will not adhere to one another, just as iron does not mix with clay. And in the days of these kings the God of heaven will set up a kingdom which shall never be destroyed; and the kingdom shall not be left to other people; it shall break in pieces and consume all these kingdoms, and it shall stand forever. Inasmuch as you saw that the stone was cut out of the mountain without hands, and that it broke in pieces the iron, the bronze, the clay, the silver, and the gold – the great God has made known to the king what will come to pass after this. The dream is certain, and its interpretation is sure."

This image is a reflection on earth of something in the spirit realm – Satan and his system. The Hebrew word for image as used in Daniel 2 is *tselem,* which means "an idolatrous figure" (#6755 Strong 1995), from a "root meaning to shade; a phantom, i.e. (figuratively) illusion, resemblance; hence representative figure" (#6754 Strong 1995). That is why it takes the form of a man's body. Remember, Revelation 17 described Satan as coming from the bottomless pit, and as the eighth king and of the seven kingdoms that attack God's people. Nebuchadnezzar's dream picked up the chronology of history midstream. Beginning with his kingdom at about 586 B.C., his dream formed a timeline of how Satan's evil governmental influence would move the empires of man to attack God's people in repeated attempts to thwart God. The successive empires would be Babylon, Medo-Persia, Greece, and Rome. Rome would become divided into two legs – east and west. The religion sanctioned by the empire also divided as well into eastern and western halves, both indelibly stamped by Constantine's doctrinal changes.

The Roman Empire disappeared into the mists of time well before the end of the age – or did it? Revelation holds the secrets. The Roman Empire was the tool Satan used to put to death Christ, the second Adam. After Christ's death and resurrection, the war between good and evil took on a whole new dimension. The war continued from the splitting apart and dissolution of the Roman Empire until the end of the age, symbolized by ten toes composed of iron and clay. The Book of Revelation takes us through the veil separating the physical and spiritual realms to witness spiritual warfare and the ultimate destiny of planet earth. By the time the war concludes, the earth will have become a very fruitful garden indeed, as we shall see.

8
The Woman Down Through Time

This chapter will put to use all that we have established to this point. The concept of prophetic times and seasons is straight out of the mind of God. The Bible repeatedly utilizes and refers to a calendar that applies to His use of days and years, times and seasons. The solar- or lunar-based calendar hanging on your wall will help in understanding prophetic time but is absolutely no substitute for it. Every culture and nation around the world attaches meaning and significance to certain dates on the calendar. When we study prophetic time, it is important to set aside our own emotions and preconceived ideas in order to hear what God's voice has to say about His prophetic times and seasons. We will listen to God's word prove His points. Now we will go back to Revelation 12:6-17 and apply some spiritual analysis:

"Then the woman fled into the wilderness, where she has a place prepared by God, that they should feed her there one thousand two hundred and sixty days. And war broke out in heaven: Michael and his angels fought with the dragon; and the dragon and his angels fought, but they did not prevail, nor was a place found for them in heaven any longer…" Remember, we read earlier in verses 1-5 that the dragon and his angels tried to devour Christ, but He was caught up to the Father's throne in heaven. After the resurrection of Christ, a battle took place in heaven beginning sometime soon after about 30 A.D. "So the great dragon was cast out, that serpent of old, called the Devil and Satan, who deceives the whole world…" At this point, let's accept what God says – the *whole world* was deceived. That leaves no one out. "…he was cast to the earth, and his angels were cast out with him. Then I heard a loud voice saying in heaven, 'Now salvation, and strength, and the kingdom of God, and the power of His Christ have come, for the accuser of our brethren, who accused them before our God day and night, has been cast down. And they overcame him by the blood of the Lamb and by the word of their testimony, and they did not love their lives to the death. Therefore rejoice, O heavens, and you who dwell in them! Woe to the inhabitants of earth and the sea! For the devil has come down to you, having great wrath, because he knows that he has a short time.'"

We see that shortly after Christ's resurrection, Satan and his demons were cast out of heaven to the earth. From this point on, evil has had no access to heaven. This event marked the beginning of the end for Satan's realm because Christ had qualified to replace Satan as ruler over the earth. The battle was now joined between Satan and the woman who had fled into the wilderness. She is composed of people who have the power to overcome Satan's realm through the use of Christ's shed blood. Unlike Adam and Eve and their descendants for whom the wages of sin is death (Romans 6:23), these people can have Christ's atoning blood cover their sins when they repent. From Satan's point of view, there were now people formed of the dust of the earth that would be very difficult to defeat. God's curse on Satan back in Genesis 3 took on a whole new significance, so Satan was very angry. Continuing with verse 13: "Now when the dragon saw that he had been cast to the earth, he persecuted the woman who gave birth to the male Child. But the woman was given two wings of a great eagle, that she might fly into the wilderness to her place, where she is nourished for a time and times and half a time, from the presence of the serpent. So the serpent spewed water out of his mouth like a flood after the woman, that he might cause her to be carried away by the flood. But the earth helped the woman, and the earth opened its mouth and swallowed up the flood which the dragon spewed out of his mouth. And the dragon was enraged with the woman, and he went to make war with the rest of her offspring, who keep the commandments of God and have the testimony of Jesus Christ."

This woman is none other than the true followers of Christ who keep His commandments. In a direct parallel to creation week in Genesis, they possess the light of God's truth to which they testify, even in the face of death. They also form the dry land (soil) for God's garden as differentiated from the vast sea of mankind. That is why verse 12 said, "Woe to the inhabitants of earth and the sea." The human race is often spoken of as "the sea of mankind."

This special woman was given the two wings of a great

eagle so she could "fly" into the wilderness to a place where she is "nourished for a time and times and half a time." This eagle, as we will see a bit later, is probably the archangel Michael who feeds the Church. He brings God's food in the form of spiritual messages – inspiration and understanding of the Scriptures of truth as we saw in Daniel chapters 2 and 10. God clearly says that this all takes place hidden from the world's view (in the wilderness, as it were) for a time, times, and half a time. We will gather scriptural information on this time period and then on the woman.

It is the same woman spoken of throughout chapter 12. Therefore the feeding in the wilderness for 1260 days mentioned in verse 6 is the same as being nourished for a time, times, and half a time. Now things get very interesting. We need to compare timing mechanisms on God's spiritual clock.

A clock keeps track of a twenty-four-hour day. Yet one can, on the same clock, keep track of hours, minutes, and seconds, knowing that they all add up to the same twenty-four-hour day. By adding weeks and months, we can determine seasons, years, centuries, and millenniums. So it is with spiritual or prophetic time. Today we do not understand every aspect of physical time keeping – atomic clocks, Greenwich Mean Time, the effect of the speed of light on time, etc. – but we can still use a clock and calendar. So it is with prophetic time. However, just because we cannot comprehend all the intricacies of spiritual time does not mean we cannot use our clock and calendar. We certainly can, and the Bible tells us how.

Comparing Physical and Spiritual Time

Most of the world uses, or at least is familiar with, the Gregorian calendar which is solar based, meaning it is based on earth's movement in relation to the sun. This calendar has divided the history of human experience into two halves: before Christ and after Christ, B.C. and A.D. The birth of Christ is the center point of time. From that center point, we can count backward to a particular date B.C. or go forward to note a date A.D. God's prophetic calendar works the same way with key events noted. See Figure 1.

/_____BC_____Christ_____A.D._____\

Figure 1

Since a calendar is cyclical, based on a circular pattern of events, important dates can be memorialized so they can be observed yearly. Physical calendars are typically backward-looking. They remind us to observe significant past events of religious or secular nature. These holy days and holidays are inserted into the yearly cycle on or about the date they occurred in history. God's calendar does this as well, but since it is also prophetic, it has the added dimension of looking forward to future events.

God's calendar also utilizes the second principle discussed in Chapter 3 on former and latter fulfillments to help us understand and prepare for the future. This unique feature allows us to study time B.C. to learn about events occurring A.D. – after Christ. As best we can, we will build a replica of God's calendar.

The overall calendar of God pictures creation "week," being seven days long. What God accomplished in seven days back in Genesis chapter one pictured the overall plan of God, which would take seven thousand years to complete. Scripture tells us in II Peter 3:8 and Psalm 90:1-4 that with God a thousand years is like a day. God knew it would take seven millenniums to accomplish His goals, with the last millennium being one thousand years of peace without Satan's influence. The first six thousand years would be a difficult time for the human race. God determined that He would work with the earth's soil through three epochs of time, which we covered in Chapter 4. The overall timeline of history could be configured like Figure 2.

Genesis

Patriarchs	Ancient Israel	Christian era	Millennium of peace
/_____2,000_____/_____2,000_____Christ_____2,000 years_____1,000 years_____\			
years	years		

/_____7,000 years_____\

creation week

Figure 2

During the second epoch, God actually told ancient Israel, through Moses, what His calendar of events would be. Israel lived through them exactly. God tied these key events to holy days that He placed on a cyclical yearly calendar. God had decreed that they would occur during the two-thousand-year-long second epoch. This is a crucial fact to understand because these events would repeat themselves in a very remarkable way in the third two-thousand-year epoch.

God called His holy days "feasts," often translated from the Hebrew word *mowed*, "an appointment, i.e. a fixed time or season; specifically a festival; conventionally a year; by implication an assembly (as convened for a definite purpose); technically the congregation; by extension the place of meeting" (#4150 Strong 1995), as a predetermined signal. If that definition sounds familiar, it is because we learned about it in Chapter 6. *Mowed* was used by God in Genesis 1:14-15 to say that the sun, moon, and stars would be used to establish signs and seasons, days and years.

There is yet a third way *mowed* has been translated from Hebrew consistent with its definition. That term is "congregation," as in congregation of Israel. Therefore God's holy days - *mowed* - were to be observed by His chosen congregation - *mowed* - to be observed in their seasons - *mowed*! The word is interchangeable because what the congregation did on those days was meant to be a prophetic sign of future events in God's plan to deliver mankind. The congregation of Israel was the "woman" He chose to work in the garden with Him until Christ's birth, death, and resurrection. Then a second congregation would be formed into a woman to assist the second Adam, Christ, in His plan to deliver the human race from the serpent's tyranny! We need to insert those days into God's timeline. That timeline looking backward from Christ's birth would look like Figure 3 with the seasons duly noted.

SEASONS OF OLD TESTAMENT CONGREGATION

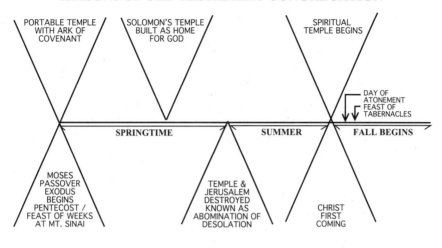

Figure 3

Now we need to verify this calendar in Scripture. Exodus 12:1-3, 5-7, 12-17: "Now the Lord spoke to Moses and Aaron in the land of Egypt, saying, 'This month shall be your *beginning* of *months*; it shall be the first month of the year to you'" (emphasis added). This month includes the Passover and Days of Unleavened Bread, which are commemorated in the spring. It would correspond to late March or April on the Gregorian calendar. In Hebrew this month is called *Nisan*. Let's continue with verse 3: "Speak to all the congregation of Israel, saying: 'On the tenth of this month every man shall take for himself a lamb, according to the house of his father, a lamb for a household... Your lamb shall be without blemish, a male of the first year... Now you shall keep it until the fourteenth day of the same month. Then the whole assembly of the congregation of Israel shall kill it at twilight. And they shall take some of the blood and put it on the doorposts and on the lintels of the houses where they eat it.'" Verses 12-17: "For I will pass through the land of Egypt on that night, and will strike all the firstborn in the land of Egypt, both man and beast; and against all the gods [demon rulers] of Egypt I will execute judgment: I am the Lord. Now the blood shall be a *sign* for you on the houses where you are. And when I see the blood, I will pass over you; and the plague shall not be on you to destroy you when I strike the land of Egypt. So this day shall be to you a memorial; and you shall keep it as a feast to the Lord throughout your generations. You shall keep it as a feast by an everlasting ordinance. Seven days you shall eat unleavened bread. On the first day you shall remove leaven from your houses... On the first day there shall be a holy convocation, and on the seventh day there shall be a holy convocation for you. No manner of work shall be done on them... So you shall observe the Feast of Unleavened Bread."

God's yearly calendar begins with the Passover and seven Days of Unleavened Bread which commemorate the awesome time in Israel and Judah's history when they were freed from bondage to Egypt. Leviticus 23 goes on to outline the rest of the holy days God wanted them to commemorate on a yearly basis.

Each annual holy day, its establishment in Leviticus 23, and the month in which it occurs are in Table 1. In the extreme right-hand column are more corroborating Scriptures.

	Feast or Holy Day	Lev. 23	Hebrew Month	Gregorian Month	Additional Scriptures
1	Passover	:5	Nisan / Abib	March or April	Exodus 13:4
2	Unleavened Bread	:6-8	Nisan / Abib	March or April	
3	Pentecost (Feast of Weeks)	:15-22	Sivan	May or June	Esther 8:9
4	Feast of Trumpets	:23-25	Tishri	September or October	I Kings 8:2
5	Day of Atonement	:26-32	Tishri	September or October	Leviticus 25:9
6	Feast of Tabernacles	:33-43	Tishri	September or October	
7	Last Great Day	:36	Tishri	September or October	

Table 1

These are the only holy days (along with the weekly Sabbath) that God has commanded to be observed. They should not be confused with other observances such as Hanukah, found on modern Jewish calendars. No other holy days have been instituted by God, nor can they be found in Scripture. That includes Christmas, Easter, and All Souls Day, but more about that later.

There are a few very important facts to note. God's calendar begins in the spring when new life begins to sprout and bud. Considering that the earth is God's garden and He is a farmer, that makes sense. In contrast, the Gregorian calendar begins at the stroke of midnight December 31st during the dead of winter.

The second thing to note is that all of God's holy days take place in the first seven months of His year. That means that they conclude in the fall just as the agricultural year does. Another way to put it is that they coincide with the seasons. Just as a farmer plants seed in the spring, intending to harvest a crop in the fall, so does God. Therefore, hidden in the seasons and the holy days is God's master plan for the human race. God intends for the entire earth to be a fruitful garden for Him. His designated holy days depict where we are in time as the seasons progress. God's holy days take us on a journey toward deliverance. They are indicators of where we are in time and are determined by the interaction of what the sun, moon, and stars represent. The holy days picture predetermined assemblies when the sun (Jesus Christ) and the moon (His congregation, His chosen woman, His helpmate) get together to accomplish something of significance on the way toward the world's deliverance. Table 2 links the holy days with the events they picture.

Holy Day	Description	New Testament Reference
Passover	Christ's death and shed blood for forgiveness of sin	Luke 22:14-20, John 13:1-5, 14-15, I Corinthians 5:7
Feast of Unleavened Bread	Overcoming sin after baptism	I Corinthians 5:8, Romans 6:4
Feast of Weeks or Pentecost	Firstfruits of God's garden receive Holy Spirit	Acts 2:1-4, Romans 8:23, James 1:18, Revelation 14:4
Feast of Trumpets	Coming of Christ and resurrection of firstfruits to free mankind from Satan	Matthew 24:30-31, I Thessalonians 4:16-17, Revelation 11:15
Day of Atonement	Mankind set free and reconciled to God. Satan and demons held accountable	Revelation 20:1-3
Feast of Tabernacles	A millennium of peace on earth	Revelation 20:4,6
Last Great Day	Resurrection of all who have died without redemption from sin	Revelation 20:5, I Corinthians 15:22, Matthew 12:41-42

Table 2

When viewed with an open mind, it is clear that these "old fashioned" Hebrew holy days have real modern significance. Look up the Scripture references and verify this important fact for yourself. God's holy days will never lose significance, for it is He who designated them to be observed. Remember that Hebrew word *mowed* stands for feast day, congregation, and seasons. We have also covered that at the very beginning in Genesis 1, the sun and moon and stars would be for signs (Hebrew *owth*) and seasons (Hebrew *mowed*). Signs are the evidence pointing to what time of the year the congregation should assemble to acknowledge events in God's plan. As a matter of fact, the word "congregation" in the Old Testament comes from the Hebrew word *mowed* about half the time. Most of the rest of the time it is translated from the Hebrew *edah* (#5712 Strong 1995), which essentially means a stated assembly of a family or group as a witness, to testify to the significance of the holy day.

Holy Days Are the Nucleus of True Signs and Wonders

When God established His holy days, He established the main signs and wonders to look for down through time. In their fulfillment, He provided the skeleton that would carry the flesh of His whole plan to deliver mankind from evil.

The holy days pinpoint those times when heaven and earth would interact, the key events taking place along the way toward the liberation of mankind. In other words they are the main signs and wonders God would use to communicate with mankind. God has been constrained by the fact that He has had to work with mere mortals in their fight against powerful, unseen foes. God chose to work with mankind while letting them use the marvelous gift of free will that He had given them. This means He had to start small and move slowly, always letting people choose good over evil, obedience over rebellion.

The fact is that mankind's struggles are ultimately spiritual. What is spiritual cannot be seen, so God uses physical people, places, times, things, and events to convey spiritual understanding. The logical conclusion is that the holy days which God proscribed and the people whom He has called to keep them are for signs and wonders. Isaiah 8:16-18 sums this up perfectly: "Bind up the testimony, seal the law among the disciples. And I will wait on the Lord, who hides His face from the house of Jacob; and I will hope in Him. Here am I and the children whom the Lord has given me! We are for signs and wonders…"

God warns us to honor no substitutes in verses 19-20: "And when they say to you, 'Seek those who are mediums and wizards, who whisper and mutter,' should not a people seek their God? Should they seek the dead on behalf of the living? To the law and to the testimony [God's word]! If they do not speak according to this word, it is because there is no light in them." Verses 21-22 warn of the end result of deception, which has certainly proven true over time: "They will pass through it hard pressed and hungry; and it shall happen, when they are hungry, that they will be enraged and curse their king and their God, and look upward. Then they will look to the earth, and see trouble and darkness, gloom of anguish; and they will be driven into darkness." The fulfillment is all about us today, as theological and secular experts look to the conditions of earth and give us a constant drumbeat of doom and gloom. One of

Satan's most effective methods used to deceive is to substitute fakes for God's real signs wherever and whenever he can.

9
The Prophetic Calendar

Physical calendars were invented when people noticed that the seasons repeat themselves annually. Let's look at a quote from the 1983 edition *World Book Encyclopedia* on the subject of the calendar:

"Calendar is a system of measuring and recording the passage of time. A major scientific advance was made when people realized that nature furnishes a regular sequence of seasons. The seasons governed their lives, determined their needs, and controlled the supply of their natural foods. They needed a calendar so they could prepare for winter before it came.

"Before the invention of the clock, people had to rely on nature's time keepers – the sun, the moon, and the stars. The daily apparent rotation of the sun provided the simplest and most obvious unit, the solar day. The seasons roughly indicated the length of another simple unit, the solar year. Early people were not aware of the fundamental cause of the seasons, the earth's revolution around the sun. But it was easy to see the changing position and shape of the moon. As a result, most ancient calendars used the interval between successive full moons, the lunar month, as an intermediate measure of time. The moon bridged the gap between the solar day and the solar year.

"The lunar month, we now know, is about 29 1/2 days long. Twelve such months amount to about 354 days. This interval is almost 11 days shorter than the true solar year which has 365 days, 5 hours, 48 minutes, and 46 seconds."

The solar system provides the ideal mechanism for keeping track of time here on earth. The earth's rotation, the moon's monthly cycle, and their revolutions around the sun are like the movements of a fine timepiece. They accurately keep track of days, weeks, and years. They form the basis for calendars that hang on walls around the world. Mankind long ago discovered that the yearly cycle is broken up into four seasons. Human survival depends upon the recurring seasons because they determine when to work the soil, plant, and harvest.

Principle 2 in Chapter 3 established that the physical and spiritual realms parallel each other. Recall what we read in Romans 1 verse 20: "… since the creation of the world His [God's] invisible attributes are clearly seen, being understood by the things that are made, even His eternal power and Godhead…" The word "Godhead" means His divine nature or mind. By applying Romans 1:20, we can conclude that the same creation used to keep track of physical time can also be used to keep track of spiritual "time" – if we know how. By employing Principle 1, which is to let the Bible interpret itself, we can assemble God's thoughts on spiritual time-keeping. Since spiritual time-keeping is used mainly for looking forward, we will call it "prophetic time."

God designed our solar system so that He could provide a way to use the sun and moon "for signs and seasons, and for days and years" (Genesis 1:14). Just as the sun and moon can keep track of the passing of time in correlation to the seasons, so does God's prophetic calendar. The 360 degrees of a circle and God's holy days keep track of the passage of spiritual seasons. This concept is right out of the mind of God and with His help can be used to decipher many prophetic passages in the Bible. The overarching principle to prophetic time-keeping is that God is working with the human race through a set of four seasons. Earth's natural, seasonal rhythms annually reflect God's grand design. God's holy days help us pinpoint where we are on the prophetic calendar of events, each event occurring in its season.

Our modern way of life has removed most people from close contact with the earth and its seasonal rhythms. Our lifestyle relegates the seasons to changes in wardrobes and a succession of different sports. The few among us who still farm as a way of life are much more aware of the seasonal progression. The farmer's year begins in the spring when he plants his fields. From spring until the end of summer, he tends his crops and waits patiently for the harvest. He watches as the sun and rain work with seed, soil, and plant in order to bear fruit. He keeps the weeds and pests at bay and the soil worked.

In Chapter 7 we covered how the earth is God's garden

and how He has a woman helping Him work it. This means that God Himself is a master gardener, a spiritual farmer. Farmer and helpmate work together patiently until the crops are ready. James 5:7-8 describes this process well: "Therefore be patient, brethren, until the coming of the Lord. See how the farmer waits for the precious fruit of the earth, waiting patiently for it until it receives the early and latter rain. You also be patient. Establish your hearts, for the coming of the Lord is at hand."

In Chapter 6 we looked into the essence of time by defining some key words in Genesis 1:14. We found that "signs and seasons" pointed to the prophetic calendar and "days and years" to the physical calendar. Recall that the sun and moon can be used for both prophetic and physical time-keeping. When the prophetic time is being observed, the sun and moon take on additional spiritual significance. The sun represents God's Son, Jesus Christ, and the moon, His people. Now we will use God's word to build His own case for the use of His prophetic calendar.

Evidence of Prophetic Time

Just as mankind first noticed the seasons and the fact that they recur, we must determine that spiritual seasons do exist and that they are tied to spiritual agriculture. Many, many Scriptures support this concept, but the following are a few to consider:

Acts 1:6-9: "Therefore, when they had come together, they asked Him, [The apostles asked Christ] saying, 'Lord, will you at this time restore the kingdom to Israel?' and He said to them, 'It is not for you to know times or seasons which the Father has put in His own authority.'"

Matthew 9:38 refers to God the Father as "Lord of the harvest."

Genesis 8:22: "While the earth remains, seedtime and harvest, cold and heat, winter and summer, and day and night shall not cease."

Ecclesiastes 3:1: "To everything there is a season, a time for every purpose under heaven."

I Thessalonians 5:1-2: "But concerning the times and the

seasons, brethren, you have no need that I should write to you. For you yourselves know perfectly that the day of the Lord so comes as a thief in the night."

Revelation 14:15: "And another angel came out of the temple, crying with a loud voice to Him who sat on the cloud, 'Thrust in Your sickle and reap, for the time has come for You to reap, for the harvest of the earth is ripe.'"

We can clearly see that God has seasons and harvests of a spiritual nature. There is no way we could possibly understand what He is getting at if we did not have annual seasons and harvests on earth. The effort a farmer must exert on the land in the correct season directly parallels how God is "farming the earth."

Now we can combine what we have learned in Figure 4, so we can actually see the prophetic calendar manifest itself. We will combine the following:

1. God's use of seasons
2. God's holy days
3. Principle of dual fulfillment, that is, a former fulfillment prior to the coming of Christ and a latter fulfillment after the coming of Christ
4. Timelines already utilized in this book

God's Overall Seasons

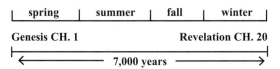

Former and Latter Fulfillment

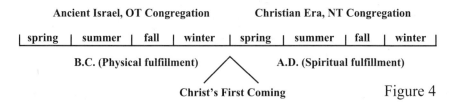

Figure 4

70

The physical calendar goes round and round in a circle, constantly repeating itself, yet ever moving forward in time. The prophetic calendar does exactly the same thing. Every year, the passing of time is observed as days, weeks, months, and seasons with special holidays carefully noted. On a physical calendar such days as Christmas, Easter, or Ramadan etc. are noted. On the prophetic calendar, God's holy days are noted in their appropriate months and seasons. See Figure 5. (We have oriented Figures 5 and 6 as the typical Gregorian calendar with the beginning of the year at the top.)

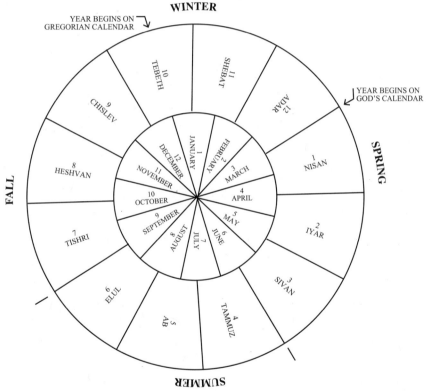

Figure 5

Now we will take the information we compiled in Chapter 8 regarding God's holy days and when they occur in the year, and we will place them on our circular calendar. See Figure 6. Notice how the holy days correspond to the agricultural growing season. Also notice that three major seasonal activities surround the holy days: planting, spring harvesting, and the fall harvest of the summer crops.

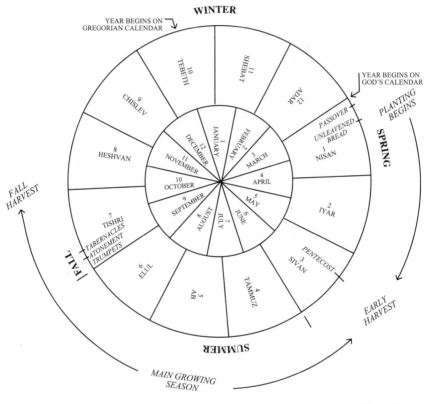

Figure 6

We are now ready to take what we have learned and interface it with God's prophetic calendar. Keep in mind that by averaging the length of the solar calendar (365.25 days) and the lunar calendar (354.37 days) we arrive at almost exactly 360 days. 360 degrees is how we measure a circle. On a physical calendar the days, weeks, and months repeat themselves over and over in a circular pattern. That is why watches and clocks go round and round in a circle to measure days. On that circular calendar man inserts the days that are important to him. God inserts the days He calls holy days and then transfers them to His prophetic calendar, so we can "see" them and note their forward progress. This allows us to determine where we are in prophetic time. Figure 7 depicts God's prophetic calendar in its most basic format. Now we turn the diagram to show a left-to-right progression of the seasons, so that we can better show time advancing forward. This orientation also corresponds with the earth's natural cycle. When it is spring and summer in the Northern Hemisphere, it is fall and winter in the South. Later on, this will help us visualize how creation reflects God's thinking.

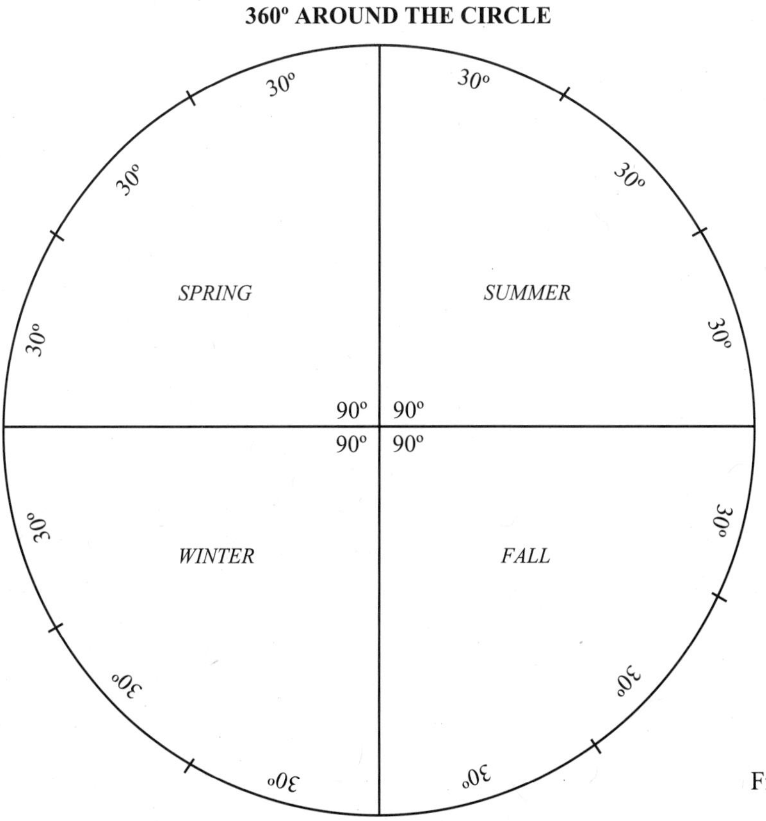

360° AROUND THE CIRCLE

Figure 7

Figure 8 now plugs God's holy days in their appropriate seasons. Notice how each season is comprised of 90 degrees. Each season can then be divided into three prophetic months with each day represented as a degree. This means a prophetic year is composed of 12 prophetic months of 30 days each. It is important to realize that God's seasons differ in length when compared to the physical year. For instance, the length of God's spring takes more physical time to accomplish than His summer season. As we progress, it will become clear why.

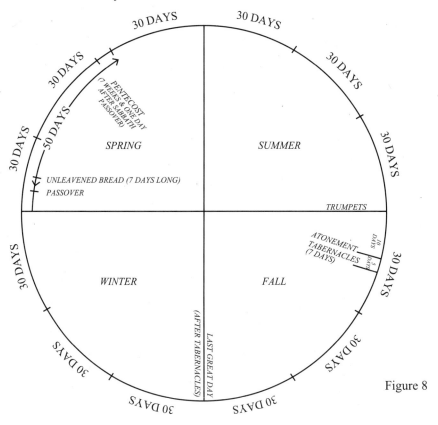

Figure 8

Now we can employ Principle 3 – that of dual fulfillment. Figure 9 will divide God's overall prophetic calendar into two halves. The first half is the history of how ancient Israel progressed from coming out of Egypt at Passover until Christ's first coming on or near the Feast of Trumpets, which occurs in early fall. The rest of the fall holy days, Atonement and Feast of Tabernacles are awaiting their fulfillment. That is why you will not find them on the Old Testament circle in Figure 9. Ancient Israel was the woman who labored until Christ's birth. Christ's coming provided a second fulfillment of Passover and began the spiritual second fulfillment of the holy days. The New Testament Church then became the woman He was working with (Revelation 12:1-5).

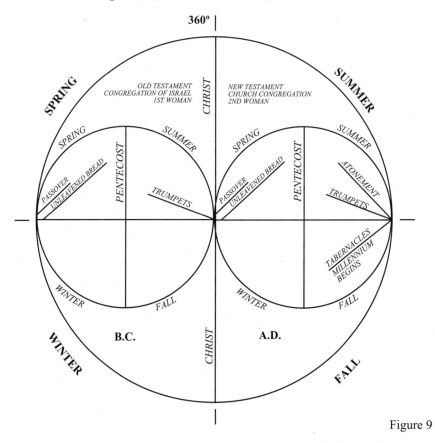

Figure 9

We have already established that God's holy days are determined by the moon. We have also learned that they are composed of specific lengths of time. For example, Passover is for one day, and Unleavened Bread takes seven days, as does the Feast of Tabernacles. Nearly an entire season elapses between Passover and Pentecost, and between Pentecost and Trumpets. From Passover to Pentecost is spring time. God calls Pentecost by two other names: the Feast of Firstfruits and the Feast of Weeks. The reason for this name is because seven weeks must be counted off from the Sabbath day which lands during the week of Unleavened Bread to Pentecost. This total passage of time equals fifty days. Pentecost means to count fifty. Seven weeks of seven days equals forty-nine days, the next day being the fiftieth day.

Hebrew Meaning of the Feast of Weeks

The Hebrew for Feast of Weeks is *mowed* (#4150 Strong 1995) of *shabuwa* (#7620 Strong 1995). *Shabuwa* means to be sevened, i.e. a week, specifically a week of years. On the physical calendar the Jews calculate seven weeks until Pentecost. The Feast of Weeks also means seven weeks of years, or forty-nine years. Pentecost/Feast of Weeks has great significance on the prophetic calendar, which we will discuss in Chapter 10. For right now we will learn how to calculate it.

Seven weeks of prophetic years may be expressed as:

7 X 360 degrees = 2520

7 X 360 = seven circles

This is shown on Figure 10.

In Chapter 10 we will examine what this period of time encompassed and the prophecies that address it.

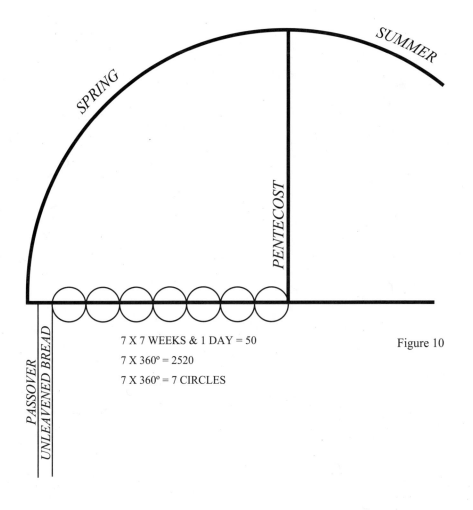

SPRING

SUMMER

PENTECOST

PASSOVER

UNLEAVENED BREAD

7 X 7 WEEKS & 1 DAY = 50

7 X 360° = 2520

7 X 360° = 7 CIRCLES

Figure 10

10
Prophecy Comes Alive

Since the period of time from Passover until Pentecost has a former and latter fulfillment, we should be able to see how this is accomplished in both the Old and New Testaments. It is easy to find the common starting point for both fulfillments. In Chapter 3 our first example of dual fulfillment was Passover, and indeed it is the place to start. Let's go back to that first Passover through to Pentecost, and then cross reference this with the New Testament.

Passover was the first holy day to occur in the history of ancient Israel. It took place with the killing of a lamb on the fourteenth day of the first month in springtime. That very night, Israel was released from captivity from Egypt. Thus began the first Passover and week of Unleavened Bread. From the Sabbath that fell in that week, the first Pentecost landed forty-nine days later, seven weeks of seven days.

On the first Pentecost the famous incident at Mount Sinai took place in which God made direct contact with ancient Israel and formed a covenant. We will quote several Scriptures from Exodus 19, breaking in at verse 4 with God speaking: "'You have seen what I did to the Egyptians, and how I bore you on eagles' wings and brought you to Myself. Now therefore, if you will obey My voice and keep My covenant, then you shall be a special treasure to Me above all people; for all the earth is Mine. And you shall be to Me a kingdom of priests and a holy nation. These are the words which you shall speak to the children of Israel.' So Moses came and called for the elders of the people, and laid before them all these words which the Lord commanded him. Then all the people answered together and said, 'All that the Lord has spoken we will do.' So Moses brought back the words of the people to the Lord."

Three days later the contract was ratified in verses 16-20: "Then it came to pass on the third day, in the morning, that there were thunderings and lightnings, and a thick cloud on the mountain; and the sound of the trumpet was very loud, so that all the people who were in the camp trembled, and Moses brought this people out of the camp to meet God, and they stood at the foot of the mountain. Now Mount Sinai was completely in smoke, because the Lord *descended upon it in fire*. Its smoke ascended like the smoke of a furnace, and the whole mountain quaked greatly. And when the blast of the trumpet sounded long and became louder and louder, Moses spoke, and God answered him by voice. Then the Lord came down upon Mount Sinai, on the top of the mountain. And the Lord called Moses to the top of the mountain, and Moses went up" (emphasis added).

Then after uttering the Ten Commandments to which the people were to agree, the reaction of the people to this awesome sight is recorded in Exodus 20 verses 18-19: "Now all the people witnessed the thunderings, the lightning flashes, the sound of the trumpet, and the mountain smoking; and when the people saw it, they trembled and stood afar off. Then they said to Moses, 'You speak with us, and we will hear, but let not God speak to us, lest we die.'"

The New Testament Fulfillment

It is important to establish that Christ died on the cross as our Passover Lamb for the remission of sin. Let's begin in I Corinthians 5:7, which not only references Christ this way but also speaks about the purpose of the Days of Unleavened Bread: "Therefore purge out the old leaven, that you may be a new lump, since you truly are unleavened. For indeed Christ, our Passover, was sacrificed for us."

Luke chapter 22 recounts the events leading up to Christ's death on the cross as our Passover. After securing the upper room to share the last supper, Christ made some astounding statements in verses 14-20: "When the hour had come, He sat down, and the twelve apostles with Him. Then He said to them, 'With fervent desire I have desired to eat this Passover with you before I suffer; for I say to you, I will no longer eat of it until it is fulfilled in the kingdom of God.' Then He took the cup, and gave thanks, and said,

'Take this and divide it among yourselves; for I say to you, I will not drink of the fruit of the vine, until the kingdom of God comes.' And He took bread, gave thanks and broke it, and gave it to them saying, 'This is My Body which is given for you; do this in remembrance of Me.' Likewise He also took the cup after supper, saying, 'This cup is the new covenant in My blood, which is shed for you.'" The next day He was crucified and died just before the Days of Unleavened Bread were to begin.

Christ laid in the grave three days and three nights and then He appeared to His disciples for forty days as recorded in Acts 1 verse 3: "To whom He also presented Himself alive after His suffering by many infallible proofs, being seen by them during forty days and speaking of the things pertaining to the kingdom of God." At the very end of this forty-three day period He appeared to them one final time before His ascension. He told the disciples to stay in Jerusalem until they would receive the Holy Spirit on Pentecost, which was fifty days after the Sabbath following the Passover of Christ's death.

The Easter Question

The Council of Nicea was called by order of the Roman Emperor Constantine in 325 A.D. Constantine, who had converted to Christianity, wanted to unify and stabilize his crumbling empire. He felt that the best way to do so would be to bring the entire empire under the umbrella of a state-backed religion. His problem was that the church he now attended was very divided along doctrinal lines. The council was convened to settle the differences with Constantine as arbiter. One of the arguments he settled was whether the church would observe Passover or Easter as a holy day.

Constantine ruled in favor of Easter in part because he did not want to be seen as favoring the Jews with whom Rome had fought many times, even though Jesus Christ, His disciples, and most early converts were Jewish. Secondarily, his empire was composed of many nationalities and ethnic groups already observing pagan spring fertility rites honoring various deities. The Teutonic tribes were worshipping the goddess Eostur. In the spring the Druids of Britain venerated sacred eggs, and the Germans both eggs and rabbits. Throughout the far-flung empire, variations on ancient pagan religions had similar holy days, symbols and icons.

By Constantine's decree, the state religion became a blend of pagan and Christian beliefs. These beliefs surrounded a non-biblical set of holy days totally obscuring God's prophetic calendar of events. Thus Satan succeeded in deceiving man to change times, laws, and seasons, as prophesied in Daniel 7:25. Ironically, ever since, millions of well-meaning people have lived and died on behalf of religions that honor the Bible yet whose doctrines are far removed from it. Easter, Christmas, holy icons, and relics are just some of the beliefs that are held as sacred that cannot be found or substantiated in Scripture. Here is what the Encyclopedia Britannica, Eleventh Edition, article on "Easter" has to say: "There is no indication of the observance of the Easter festival in the New Testament, or in the writings of the apostolic fathers."

As a matter of fact, the Good-Friday-to-Easter-Sunday tradition contradicts Christ's death as the Passover Lamb who would lie in the grave for three days and three nights (Matthew 12:38-40). Protestant scholars working on the King James Version went so far as to substitute the word "Easter" for "Passover" in Acts 12:4. This word (#3957 Strong 1995) is translated "Easter" only in this verse. It is translated "Passover" in all 28 of the other places in the Bible where it is used.

This is the exchange between Christ and His disciples at the last appearance before Pentecost in Acts 1 verses 4-9: "And being assembled together with them, He commanded them not to depart from Jerusalem, but to wait for the Promise of the Father, 'which,' He said, 'you have heard from Me; for John [John the Baptist] truly baptized with water, but you shall be baptized with the Holy Spirit not many days from now.' Therefore, when they had come together, they asked Him, saying, 'Lord, will you at this time restore the kingdom to Israel?' And he said to them, 'It is not for you to know times or seasons which the Father has put in His own authority. But you shall receive power when the Holy Spirit has come upon you; and you shall be *witnesses* to Me in Jerusalem, and in all Judea and Samaria, and to the end of the earth.' Now when He had spoken these things, while they watched, He was taken up, and a cloud received Him out of their sight" (emphasis added). "Witnesses" has been italicized so you would take note, as we will soon be discussing this.

Acts chapter 2:1-4 continues with what did happen a week or so later on Pentecost: "When the Day of Pentecost had fully come, they were all with one accord in one place. And suddenly there came a sound from heaven, as of a rushing mighty wind, and it filled the whole house where they were sitting. Then there appeared to them divided tongues, as of fire, and one sat upon each of them. And they were all filled with the Holy Spirit and began to speak with other tongues, as the Spirit gave them utterance."

This Pentecost of the New Testament is cross referenced to the Pentecost at Mount Sinai in Hebrews 12 verses 18-19: "For you have not come to the mountain that may be touched and that burned with fire, and to blackness and darkness and tempest, and the sound of a trumpet and the voice of words, so that those who heard it begged that the word should not be spoken to them anymore." Continuing in verses 22-24: "But you have come to Mount Zion and to the city of the living God, the heavenly Jerusalem, to an innumerable company of angels, to the general assembly and church of the firstborn who are registered in heaven, to God the Judge of all, to the spirits of just men made perfect, to Jesus the Mediator of the new covenant, and to the blood of sprinkling that speaks better things than that of Abel."

Now it is evident in Scripture that the holy days indeed have two fulfillments, a prophetic duality. The first fulfillment was very obvious. It was to bear witness to and record, because it was very physical. There were smoke, fire, a shaking mountain, angelic trumpets and God's booming voice.

The second fulfillment has a much smaller physical footprint but a much larger spiritual dynamic to it. There were rushing wind, small tongues of fire, and the miraculous ability to speak in one's own language and be heard in any language. This was obviously an extraordinary experience, but not as terrifying as the first fulfillment.

Hebrews chapter 12 told us that those present at the second fulfillment had come to a spiritual Jerusalem, on a spiritual mountain of Zion. At this encounter with the divine majesty of Christ, those present received the Holy Spirit to dwell within them and were thus ratifiers of a new covenant. Therefore, those gathered on that first Pentecost after Christ's resurrection were doing something unique in history. They were standing in the physical city of Jerusalem on Mount Zion, while at the same time entering a spiritual city of Jerusalem on a spiritual version of Mount Zion. This would have been impossible for anyone to comprehend without a former physical fulfillment. But the dualities of that day did not stop there! We will read more of Acts chapter 2 and explain.

Immediately after the divine wind and fire descended on the disciples and brethren (120 people in all, as told in Acts 1:15), the disciples began to speak in other tongues as the Holy Spirit gave them utterance. Acts 2:5-8 explains this phenomenon. "And there were dwelling in Jerusalem Jews, devout men, from every nation under heaven. And when this sound occurred, the multitude came together, and were confused, because everyone heard them speak in his own language. Then they were all amazed and marveled, saying to one another, 'Look, are not all these who speak Galileans? And how is it that we hear, each in our own language in which we were born?'" Verses 9-11 list at least sixteen nationalities present. People tried to make sense of it all in verses 12-13: "So they were all amazed and perplexed, saying to one another, 'Whatever could this mean?' Others mocking said, 'They are full of new wine.'"

Peter then said some amazing things by way of explanation. We will pick up the story in Acts 2 verses 14-24: "But Peter, standing up with the eleven, raised his voice and said to them, 'Men of Judea and all who dwell in Jerusalem, let this be known to you, and heed my words. For these are not drunk, as you suppose, since it is only the third hour of the day. But this is what was spoken by the prophet Joel: "And it shall come to pass in the last days, says God, that I will pour out of My Spirit on all flesh; your sons and your daughters shall prophesy, your young men shall see visions, your old men shall dream dreams. And on My menservants and on My maidservants I will pour out My Spirit in those days; and they shall prophesy. I will show wonders in heaven above and signs in the earth beneath: blood and fire and vapor of smoke. The sun shall be turned into darkness, and the moon into blood, before the coming of the great and awesome day of the Lord. And it shall come to pass that whoever calls on the name of the Lord shall be saved." Men of Israel, hear these words: Jesus of Nazareth, a Man attested by God to you by miracles, wonders, and signs which God did through Him in your midst, as you yourselves also know – Him, being delivered by the determined purpose and foreknowledge of God, you have taken by lawless hands, have crucified, and put to death; whom God raised up, having loosed the pains of death, because it was not possible that He should be held by it.'"

Peter was revealing to the assembled crowd the meaning of what had happened, from the death of Christ on Passover fifty-three days earlier, right up to that very moment on Pentecost. His words also confirmed what we established in Chapter 6 of what the sun and moon represent.

Peter was explaining that a prophecy written by Joel in the Old Testament had been fulfilled in the past seven and a half weeks. Here is what he was attesting to in chronological order:

1. Fifty-three days ago Jesus Christ died on the cross, thus turning the Light of the Son (sun) into darkness.

2. Christ's shed blood figuratively covered the moon with blood, which means to remove the sins of the moon, the congregation of the Church.

3. Three days later He rose from the dead, giving Him power over death.

4. Now fifty days later you are seeing the signs and wonders that confirm that Jesus Christ of Nazareth was indeed the Son of God. Thus they had witnessed signs and wonders in the sun, moon, and stars in a very real yet spiritual sense.

Those present then understood that the miracles of Christ's ministry were signs in the "sun" and now they were seeing signs in the "moon." They had seen the physical signs surrounding Christ's death and could now put two and two together because of Peter's explanation. Luke 23:44-45 tells us what occurred while Christ was dying on the cross: "Now it was about the sixth hour, and there was darkness over all the earth until the ninth hour. Then the sun was darkened, and the veil of the temple was torn in two."

Now everything was making sense, so in Acts 2:37-38 many in the crowd on that first Pentecost reacted: "Now when they heard this, they were cut to the heart, and said to Peter and the rest of the apostles, 'Men and brethren, what shall we do?' Then Peter said to them, 'Repent, and let every one of you be baptized in the name of Jesus Christ for the remission of sins; and you shall receive the gift of the Holy Spirit.'" Later that day about three thousand were baptized (verse 41).

This was the very beginning of a two-thousand-year effort by the Church (symbolized by a woman) to be Christ's witness on the earth. Recall Christ's words in Acts 1:4-8 when He appeared to His disciples approximately ten days before Pentecost. At that meeting the apostles asked Christ if He was about to restore the kingdom to Israel (verse 6). Christ responded in verses 7-8: "It is not for you to know times or seasons which the Father has put in His own authority. But you shall receive power when the Holy Spirit has come upon you; and you shall be **witnesses** to Me in Jerusalem, and in all Judea and Samaria, and to the end of the earth" (emphasis added). On that first Pentecost the apostles got started in Jerusalem and would extend their preaching to surrounding areas, but to reach the whole world would take nearly two thousand more years.

The disciples had been told that it was not for them to know times and seasons. The times and seasons have now advanced far enough that they can be discerned. Speaking of our time, Christ told His disciples in Luke 21:29-33 something regarding the end of the age and His return: "Then He spoke to them a parable: 'Look at the fig tree, and all the trees. When they are already budding, you see and know for yourselves that summer is now near. So you also, when you see these things happening, know that the kingdom of God is near. Assuredly, I say to you, this generation will by no means pass away until all things take place. Heaven and earth will pass away, but My words will by no means pass away.'" Understanding God's calendar and the prophetic seasons are essential keys.

11
To Be A Witness

If you have continued reading this book up to this point, you are ready to tackle one of the most intriguing and important mysteries of the Bible - the two witnesses of Revelation 11. Do not let your mind be constrained by anything you may have heard in the past. This is a deep subject that is woven into the entire Bible; therefore it is important to listen for God's voice through His own word. If necessary, refer to Chapter 4 "The History of Spiritual Hearing." The work of the two witnesses is absolutely crucial to the preservation of this earth, but rest assured, their success is a foregone conclusion.

Most people familiar with the subject of the two witnesses think of Revelation 11, so let's read verses 1-6: "Then I was given a reed like a measuring rod. And the angel stood, saying, 'Rise and measure the temple of God, the altar, and those who worship there. But leave out the court which is outside the temple, and do not measure it, for it has been given to the Gentiles. And they will tread the holy city underfoot for forty-two months. And I will give power to my two witnesses, and they will prophesy one thousand two hundred and sixty days, clothed in sackcloth.' These are the two olive trees and the two lamp stands standing before the God of the earth. And if anyone wants to harm them, fire proceeds from their mouth and devours their enemies. And if anyone wants to harm them, he must be killed in this manner. These have power to shut heaven, so that no rain falls in the days of their prophecy; and they have power over waters to turn them to blood, and to strike the earth with all plagues, as often as they desire."

These are not two individual people that God unleashes on the earth in the last days! What we have learned from God's word about the holy days, the woman in the garden, and God's prophetic calendar will open our minds to understand this vital subject. Let us now cross reference some key Scriptures, letting the Bible unravel this mystery.

Note that they speak prophecy for 1260 days. "Prophesy" in the Greek is *propheteuo* which means "to foretell events, divine, speak under inspiration, exercise the prophetic office" (#4395 Strong 1995). These various shades of meaning allow for more than just foretelling future events. This is important to keep in mind if we are to avoid being deceived. The Bible tells us that there are no more prophecies to be written after the Bible was completed. Revelation 22:18-19 speaks to this in strong language: "For I testify to everyone who hears the words of the prophecy of this book: If anyone adds to these things, God will add to him the plagues that are written in this book; and if anyone takes away from the words of the book of this prophecy, God shall take away his part from the Book of Life, from the holy city, and from the things which are written in this book." Therefore since the final book of the Bible was written nearly two thousand years ago, there have been no other prophecies that have come from God – none! With this understanding, we will not be led astray by false prophets, astrologers, or fortune tellers. Prophecy is now confined to inspired teaching under the guidance of the Holy Spirit.

Now we need to compile more information on the two witnesses from various places in the Bible to get a more complete picture of who they are, what they do, and for how long.

The Two Witnesses

In Revelation 11:3 Christ told John, "I will give power to My two witnesses, and they will prophecy one thousand two hundred and sixty days..." Verse 6: "These have power to shut heaven, so that no rain falls in the days of their prophecy; and they have power over waters to turn them to blood, and to strike the earth with all plagues, as often as they desire." In Acts 1:8 after telling the disciples it was not for them to know times and seasons, Christ said, "'But you shall receive power when the Holy Spirit has come upon you; and you shall be witnesses to Me in Jerusalem, and in all Judea and Samaria, and to the end of the earth.'" In both Scriptures the term "witnesses" comes from the exact same Greek word *martus* (#3144 Strong 1995) meaning a witness, or figuratively by analogy a martyr. We have already covered what happened to the disciples on that first Pentecost. They received the Holy Spirit by wind and fire and were able to speak in miraculous ways, as well as explain the mysteries of God, i.e., signs in the sun and the moon, and the moon turning to blood, etc. Then they were able to baptize three thousand repentant Jews, thus turning water into blood – Christ's blood. This is the same power given to the two witnesses in Revelation 11. Therefore the power the disciples were given is the same power given to the two witnesses. This power was set to work from that first Pentecost forward for a period of 1260 prophetic days.

Let's be clear, it was the Holy Spirit dwelling in them that was the source of all of this miraculous power. The ability to explain God's mysteries, drop His rain in the form of true doctrine, and baptize into the blood of Christ to remove sin are extraordinary powers. In addition, they were also given power to spread cleansing fire from their mouths. This made the living word a cleansing force within the recipient, and it all started with the fire that the disciples received on that first Pentecost. The withholding of rain and fire allows Satan's plagues to continue to buffet people who refuse to repent or believe. In Revelation 19:10b an angel told the apostle John, "...Worship God! For the testimony of Jesus is the *spirit of prophecy*" (emphasis added). The word "testimony" is another form of the word witness, in Greek, *marturia* which means "evidence given" (#3141 Strong 1995). Therefore having the indwelling Holy Spirit makes it possible to use one's mouth to preach the truth of the Scriptures and to spread godly fire.

That first Pentecost is the perfect example. Peter was able to explain to the assembled crowd the significance of what they were seeing and hearing. By preaching from the Old Testament prophet Joel, Peter was performing the job of a witness using the living word of God from the Old Testament. The New Testament had not even been written at this point. It is an important piece of the puzzle to realize Peter was using the witness of the Old Testament, because we are about to prove that the two witnesses are the Old and New Testament.

The Two Witnesses Speak

We have covered the concept of spiritual hearing in Chapter 4. Now we need to briefly cover spiritual speech, for that is what the two witnesses are. We will now employ the concept of the physical realm helping to understand the spiritual. Physical speech requires three things: air in the form of breath, vocal chords for the breath to pass through, and a mouth to form the words. To speak spiritual truth, one needs spiritual breath. On the first Pentecost that rushing wind was the breath of God. That wind made it possible for the disciples to speak miraculously and explain the mysteries of Joel.

So the disciples would understand what was taking place, Christ had done something very unusual a few weeks before. Shortly after His resurrection from the dead, Christ appeared to the disciples. Here is what happened as recorded in John 20 verses 19-23: "Then, the same day at evening, the first day of the week, when the doors were shut where the disciples were assembled, for fear of the Jews, Jesus came and stood in the midst, and said to them, 'Peace be with you.' When He had said this, He showed them His hands and His side. Then the disciples were glad when they saw the Lord. So Jesus said to them again, 'Peace to you! As the Father has sent Me, I also send you.' And when He had said this, He breathed on them, and said to them, 'Receive the Holy Spirit. If you forgive the sins of any, they are forgiven them; if you retain the sins of any, they are retained.'"

Christ breathed on the disciples and said, "Receive the Holy Spirit," – yet nothing happened at that precise moment. Christ then tied reception of the Holy Spirit to the forgiveness of sin. This incident took place at the beginning of the forty days of His appearances to the disciples after His death and resurrection. At the end of the forty days, just before His ascension into the clouds, He gave additional information to the disciples. We have already quoted Acts 1:8 in which Christ said they would receive power to be His witnesses when the Holy Spirit would come upon them. Then on Pentecost Christ's Holy Spirit indeed entered them in the form of wind and fire. That wind was Christ's spiritual breath! This breath is what enabled them to speak the truth from the prophet Joel. The apostles went on to write the New Testament which completed the word of God to which nothing could be added or taken away.

The Bible is a living book because Christ speaks through its words. We can hear His words if we have ears to hear and want to listen. II Timothy 3:16 tells us, "All Scripture is given by inspiration of God, and is profitable for doctrine, for reproof, for correction, for instruction in righteousness...." "Inspiration" comes from the Greek word *theopneustos*, which means "divinely breathed in" (#2315 Strong 1995). The Bible is literally God's breath written on pages! That breath can enter an individual at baptism, thus making those words come alive within them. That is why the Bible can be called "the word of God." Listen to what Hebrews 4:12-13 has to say: "For the word of God is living and powerful, and sharper than any two-edged sword, piercing even to the division of soul and spirit, and of joints and marrow, and is a discerner of the thoughts and intents of the heart. And there is no creature hidden from His sight, but all things are naked and open to the eyes of Him to whom we must give account." The word lives within those who have received the Holy Spirit. To all other people the Bible is a helpful book with guidelines for life, or a history book, or a literary work. Some irreverently call the Bible a compilation of fairy tales or old wives' tales.

One of Jesus Christ's names is "the Word" which in the Greek is *Logos*, meaning something said, including the thought, and also reasoning and mental faculties (#3056 Strong 1995). *Logos* is translated "Word" in John 1:1-3. "In the beginning was the Word, and the Word was with God, and the Word was God. He was in the beginning with God. All things were made through Him, and without Him nothing was made that was made." Therefore Christ is the Word, the spirit of prophecy, and the testimony or witness of it (Revelation 19:10). In fact, Revelation 1:5 calls Christ "...the faithful witness, the firstborn from the dead, and the ruler over the kings of the earth. To Him who loved us and washed us from our sins in His own blood...."

Therefore Christ's spoken witness composes the words of the Bible, which is divided into two parts. The first or former witness is the Old Testament, and the second or latter witness is the New Testament. The two Testaments also form the former and latter rains. With Christ's indwelling breath, the truth lives within the baptized individual. Consequently the two witnesses live inside the baptized person making them a witness for Christ. The inherent power of the two witnesses comes by the Holy Spirit. This power results in the ability to start and stop the rain, spread Christ's fire, and turn water into blood. Revelation 11 said this power would be operative for 1260 prophetic days.

The two witnesses were to work from within the true Church in a two-fold commission from Christ. Christ gives this commission in Mark 16 verses 15-20: "And He said to them, 'Go into all the world and preach the gospel to every creature. He who believes and is baptized will be saved; but he who does not believe will be condemned. And these signs will follow those who believe: In My name they will cast out demons; they will speak with new tongues; they will take up serpents; and if they drink anything deadly, it will by no means hurt them; they will lay hands on the sick, and they will recover.' So then, after the Lord had spoken to them, He was received up into heaven, and sat down at the right hand of God. And they went out and preached everywhere, the Lord working with them and confirming the word through the accompanying signs. Amen."

The first part of this great commission was to preach the gospel of the kingdom. Preaching the gospel means to proclaim the good message, the good news of the kingdom of God. It is a hopeful message of peace and good will toward mankind. It is not a message of doom and gloom for the masses and hope for just a few. This good news is the theme of the two witnesses. The second part of the great commission is to baptize all who would believe and repent so their sins would be forgiven. This gospel message started out as a small work on that first Pentecost and would continue for 1260 prophetic days until it would reach the whole world. The end result was never intended to be a catastrophic climax at the end of the age, but rather the elimination of Satan's tyrannical influences. Satan is the one who wants to destroy mankind, not God.

Coupled with belief is obedience. Mark in your mind that to receive the Holy Spirit and its power and guidance one had to have been present on that first Pentecost. From that point it has been passed on down through the ages from generation to generation within the true Church. In essence, this means down through 1260 prophetic days. This is all further proof of how much God's holy days matter.

That first Pentecost marked the beginning of the spring planting season. Just as Christ had sown the seed of the word in His disciples, they were to continue sowing and watering until the springtime harvest would be complete at the end of the 1260 prophetic days. This would mark the second fulfillment of the spring holy day season – once in the Old Testament and once in the New Testament.

An incredible thing happens when we look at prophecy being fulfilled twice. Each fulfillment is only one-half of the total fulfillment. By God's calculation, Pentecost is celebrated annually by computing seven weeks of seven days or forty-nine days. Prophetically, by definition Pentecost is calculated seven times seven weeks of prophetic years, or seven times 360 which equals 2520. When each fulfillment is looked at as one-half of the total, we can divide the total of 2520 by two with the answer being 1260! Each fulfillment could also be expressed as seven half-circles of time. One-half of a circle is 180 degrees. Therefore seven times 180 also equals 1260. This number is very important in prophecy and is referred to in a number of Scriptures that we will examine in Chapter 12. The following figures will help us visualize the mathematics. See Figures 11, 12, and 13.

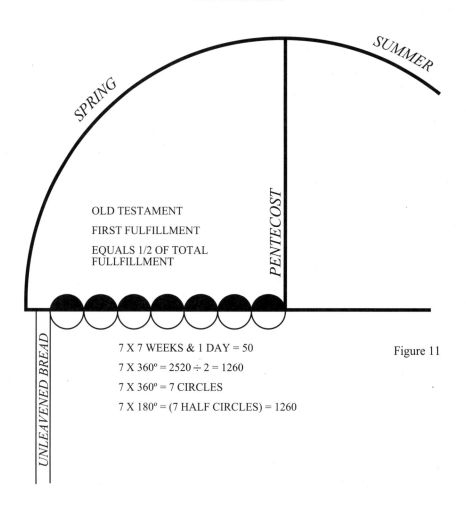

OLD TESTAMENT

SUMMER

SPRING

OLD TESTAMENT
FIRST FULFILLMENT
EQUALS 1/2 OF TOTAL
FULLFILLMENT

PENTECOST

UNLEAVENED BREAD

7 X 7 WEEKS & 1 DAY = 50

7 X 360° = 2520 ÷ 2 = 1260

7 X 360° = 7 CIRCLES

7 X 180° = (7 HALF CIRCLES) = 1260

Figure 11

96

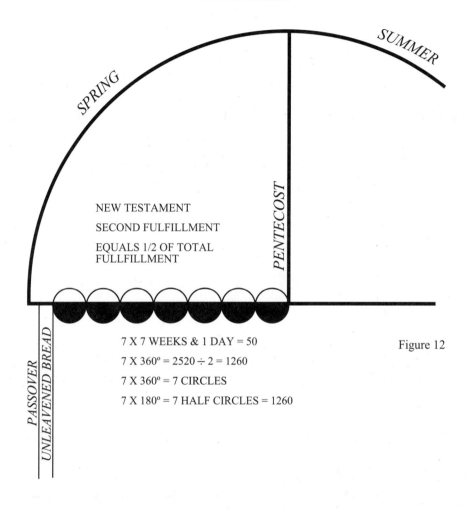

NEW TESTAMENT

SUMMER

SPRING

NEW TESTAMENT

SECOND FULFILLMENT

EQUALS 1/2 OF TOTAL
FULLFILLMENT

PENTECOST

PASSOVER
UNLEAVENED BREAD

7 X 7 WEEKS & 1 DAY = 50

7 X 360º = 2520 ÷ 2 = 1260

7 X 360º = 7 CIRCLES

7 X 180º = 7 HALF CIRCLES = 1260

Figure 12

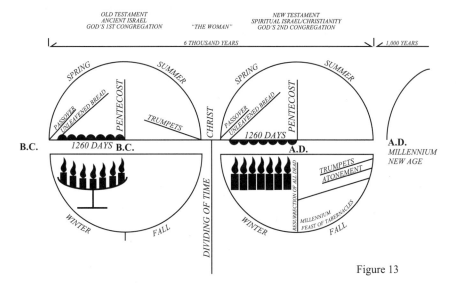

Figure 13

The Gospel of the Kingdom

Pondering how much thought and effort God has put into His plans to deliver mankind from tyranny is very humbling and very encouraging. He dearly loves the human race. God the Father and Jesus Christ have worked incredibly hard to put everything in place for the dawn of a new age of peace and harmony. His promised Millennium lies just ahead. Speaking of the Millennium, Isaiah 11:9 tells us, "They shall not hurt nor destroy in all My holy mountain, [God's kingdom] for the earth shall be full of the knowledge of the Lord as the waters cover the sea."

God is even now beginning to open ears to hear and eyes to see the many ways He is able to communicate to humanity. He speaks to us through all creation – the light of the sun, the reflected glow of the moon, flora and fauna. God's thoughts are hidden within it all. However, it is the incredible God-breathed word of the two witnesses, the Old Testament and the New Testament that opens the door of knowledge. Only the Bible can keep us on the straight path between the ditches of an atheistic view of creation or worshipping the creation itself. Within the pages of the Bible, He instructs us on how to comprehend His calendar, why His holy days are so important, how to love our fellowman, and how to love and appreciate both God the Father and the Son. All of these are brought together as the two witnesses of the good news of the gospel of the kingdom. These witnesses, penned by God's faithful servants, were given to the Church to take to the whole world as a witness before the end of Satan's evil age. No wonder Matthew 24:14 elevates the preaching of the gospel of the kingdom to the world as a witness as the chief milestone to watch for, as the signal that the end was very near. No wonder Satan hates the gospel of the kingdom so much and has tried to stop it any way he could.

To Touch the Kingdom

We can get a bit of the flavor of what it will be like in the Millennium, when Satan's tyranny is replaced by God's liberty, by seeing what it was like to be in the presence of Christ when He was on earth.

On the night of His betrayal, Christ stood before the Roman Governor Pontius Pilate. John 18:33-38 records a famous exchange between the two men in which Christ plainly says He is a king with a kingdom: "Then Pilate entered the Praetorium again, called Jesus, and said to Him, 'Are You the King of the Jews?' Jesus answered him, 'Are you speaking for yourself about this, or did others tell you this concerning Me?' Pilate answered, 'Am I a Jew? Your own nation and the chief priests have delivered You to me. What have You done?' Jesus answered, 'My kingdom is not of this world. If My kingdom were of this world, My servants would fight, so that I should not be delivered to the Jews; but now My kingdom is not from here.' Pilate therefore said to Him, 'Are you a king then?' Jesus answered, 'You say rightly that I am a king. For this cause was I born, and for this cause I have come into the world, that I should bear witness to the truth. Everyone who is of the truth hears My voice.' Pilate said to Him, 'What is truth?' And when he had said this, he went out again to the Jews, and said to them, 'I find no fault in Him at all.'"

Christ plainly stated that He is a King whose kingdom was not of this world. "World" is the English word translated from *kosmos* meaning "orderly arrangement" (#2889 Strong 1995) under the *kosmokrator* (#2888 Strong 1995), Satan the current ruler of this sad world. II Corinthians 4:4 refers to Satan as the "god of this world." Here "world" is the English word translated from the Greek *aion* meaning "an age" (#165 Strong 1995). For the six thousand years since Eden, man has lived in Satan's age under his evil influence. This arrangement will soon come to an end, and the sweet influences of Christ's kingdom will be the new order. During Christ's short ministry on earth, a sad dark world glimpsed the future, and most people loved it!

Although Christ did not look like a king, He had astonishing wisdom, authority, and power. He came into the world in a very humble way. His first night on earth was spent in a barn lying in a manger. The Son of a carpenter, He became a carpenter. He was accustomed to dirt, sweat, and toil. He was a man of such average appearance that He could slip through a crowd unnoticed (John 10:39) and was betrayed by an identifying kiss (Matthew 26:48-49). He looked so unlike a king with a kingdom that He once told the Pharisees that the approaching of the kingdom could not be observed with physical eyesight. Read the account in Luke 17 verses 20-21: "Now when He was asked by the Pharisees when the kingdom of God would come, He answered them and said, 'The kingdom of God does not come with observation; nor will they say, "See here!" or "See there!" For indeed, the kingdom of God is within you.'" "Within you" is better translated "in your midst." (See marginal reference, New King James Version of the Bible, Thomas Nelson Inc.). Matthew 4:16-17 explains that Jesus was a light to a world, living in Satan's darkness, and the light that shone from Him was the gospel of the kingdom shining from its King. "'The people who sat in darkness have seen a great light, and upon those who sat in the region and shadow of death Light has dawned.' [a quote from Isaiah 9:2] From that time Jesus began to preach and to say, 'Repent, for the kingdom of heaven is at hand.'"

Wherever Christ was, the kingdom of heaven was near to

a people who were still held in darkness by the god of this world. Although He did not look like a king, and His disciples did not look like His subjects, the people who flocked to Him by the thousands saw, experienced, and felt the effects of the kingdom of God. Everywhere He preached the gospel of the kingdom, and He performed the signs and wonders that accompany His kingdom. Demons were cast out and the sick healed (Matthew 8:14-17). The blind were given their sight, the dead were raised, and the lame made to walk (Matthew 11:5, 15:30-31).

In one way or another, all human suffering can be laid at Satan's feet. When Christ's kingdom rules the whole planet, that same power, love, and compassion will extend everywhere. For one thousand years, an entire Millennium, the earth will experience what it must have been like in the Garden of Eden. Christ passed that same healing power to His disciples by His authority when He was on earth and by His Holy Spirit from that first Pentecost after His resurrection. We have already examined that first Pentecost. Now read about the disciples' experiences as emissaries or ambassadors of God's kingdom of heaven here on earth.

Matthew 10 verses 5-15: "These twelve Jesus sent out and commanded them, saying: 'Do not go into the way of the Gentiles, and do not enter a city of the Samaritans. But rather go to the lost sheep of the house of Israel. And as you go, preach, saying, "The kingdom of heaven is at hand." Heal the sick, cleanse the lepers, raise the dead, cast out demons. Freely you have received, freely give. Provide neither gold nor silver nor copper in your money belts, nor bag for your journey, nor two tunics, nor sandals, nor staffs; for a worker is worthy of his food. Now whatever city or town you enter, inquire who in it is worthy, and stay there till you go out. And when you go into a household, greet it. If the household is worthy, let your peace come upon it. But if it is not worthy, let your peace return to you. And whoever will not receive you nor hear your words, when you depart from that house or city, shake off the dust from your feet. Assuredly, I say to you, it will be more tolerable for the land of Sodom and Gomorrah in the day of judgment than for that city!'"

Luke 10 verses 1-11: "After these things the Lord appointed seventy others also, and sent them two by two before His face into every city and place where He Himself was about to go. Then He said to them, 'The harvest truly is great, but the laborers are few; therefore pray the Lord of the harvest to send out laborers into His harvest. Go your way; behold, I send you out as lambs among wolves. Carry neither money bag, knapsack, or sandals; and greet no one along the road. But whatever house you enter, first say, "Peace to this house." And if a son of peace is there, your peace will rest on it; if not, it will return to you. And remain in the same house, eating and drinking such things as they give, for the laborer is worthy of his wages. Do not go from house to house. Whatever city you enter, and they receive you, eat such things as are set before you. And heal the sick there, and say to them, "The kingdom of God has come near to you." But whatever city you enter, and they do not receive you, go out into its streets and say, "The very dust of your city which clings to us we wipe off against you. Nevertheless know this, that the kingdom of God has come near you."'"

Luke 10 verses 17-20: "Then the seventy returned with joy, saying, 'Lord, even the demons are subject to us in Your name.' And He said to them, 'I saw Satan fall like lightning from heaven. Behold, I give you the authority to trample on serpents and scorpions, and over all the power of the enemy, and nothing shall by any means hurt you. Nevertheless do not rejoice in this, that the spirits are subject to you, but rather rejoice because your names are written in heaven.'"

God never intended to destroy the earth or its people, but rather draw them away from Satan and to Himself. His holy days depict how and when. The second fulfillment of prophecy is far along. We have passed the second fulfillment of Passover, Unleavened Bread, and Pentecost, which puts us past spring and into summer. In the summer fulfillment, we have passed the abomination of desolation and are now living through the two witnesses standing up once again. This will be quickly followed by Christ's return, pictured by the Feast of Trumpets (1335th day). Satan's kingdom is banished ten prophetic days later on the Day of Atonement (1345th day), and the start of the Millennium on the 1350th day.

The true gospel of the kingdom is composed of all the good news that prophecy, God's prophetic calendar, the holy days (including God's Sabbath), His creation, and His true signs and wonders have to tell us!

12

The Witnesses at War

The Book of Revelation is the Bible's main chronicle of spiritual warfare. Spiritual warfare, by its very nature, is not something we can see with our physical eyesight. However, we actually do see, feel, and experience its effects every day. The effects of evil influence upon the earth are rampant. Every day the news media reports on the effects of evil. God's media for reporting on the great spiritual war are the prophetic words of the Bible. God wrote down in advance how He will eradicate evil step by step, battle after battle. The holy days which God instituted represent key spiritual events. They are major tide-turning events that changed the course of history. God chose to wage war in two halves with former and latter fulfillments. This war is being fought on so many levels, in so many theaters, and on so many battlefields that its complexity is truly mind boggling. The old cliché "the fog of war" does not do justice to the confusion and complexity of spiritual warfare.

The Book of Revelation was written to help us penetrate the fog of war. Just as fog slowly lifts, burned off by the sun or pushed aside by the wind, so it is in this great war. The war will not be completely understood until it is finally over, the last foe vanquished, his last weapon thrown down. I say this that you may realize that it is far too soon to claim that the entire Bible can be understood. This also is true for the Book of Revelation itself. At the same time, however, the war is far enough along and the seasons far enough advanced that more can now be understood than ever before.

By analogy, compare the Book of Revelation to a history book written in advance. Any good history book written on a major physical war, for instance World War II, must cover all major aspects of the war. World War II had many separate sub-categories, such as the air war, naval war, and land war. Also, a good history has to deal with logistical efforts to move vast numbers of men and material.

The struggle to provide good supply lines must also be covered in the history. The war's strategy must be covered. The intelligence and espionage efforts must be covered. Also, the war effort on the home front must be covered in a good history. Each of these subdivisions of the overall war must be explained from the beginning to the end of the conflict. That requires the history text to "back up" from time to time to fill in the reader on various dynamics and how they interact. This is exactly how the Book of Revelation is written. The style of backing up in time to supply more information or to direct the reader's attention to certain subdivisions of the war is important for us to keep in mind. Remembering this will help us keep track of the chronology and history of God's war effort. Cognizance of this fact will also prove invaluable in lifting the fog of war as we connect Scripture to Scripture, letting God reveal His thoughts to us.

The Fog of War Lifts

Revelation 11:1-3 provided us two important pieces of information. The apostle John was given a reed to measure God's temple but told not to measure the court outside the temple, for it was to be trampled by the Gentiles for 42 months. Secondly, he was told that the two witnesses would prophesy, or teach, for 1260 days. We established in Chapter 9 that God's prophetic calendar has twelve months of 30 days. Therefore 42 prophetic months equals 1260 prophetic days (42 X 30 = 1,260). We can see that we are dealing with the same amount of time. During this period of time, the word in the form of the two witnesses has dwelt in the true Church waging spiritual warfare against Satan and his system. Paul advised the Church about this spiritual war with these words in Ephesians 6 verses 11-12: "Put on the whole armor of God, that you may be able to stand against the wiles of the devil. For we do not wrestle against flesh and blood, but against principalities, against powers, against the rulers of the darkness of this age, against spiritual hosts of wickedness in the heavenly [translated "high" in the King James Version] places." For 1260 prophetic days this small Church successfully battled evil by casting out demons, healing the sick, baptizing people (which turns water into blood), and preaching the gospel of the kingdom of God. They also valiantly fought to keep God's Sabbath and holy days. Revelation 11:1 told us that these people were being measured as the temple of God. The subject of the temple will be addressed a little later. Right now we want to finish with the prophetic chronology.

The next piece of information regarding the sequence of events in Revelation 11 is in verse 7. "When they [the two witnesses] finished their testimony [*marturia*, "evidence given" (#3141 Strong 1995)], the beast that ascends out of the bottomless pit will make war against them, overcome them, and kill them." Overcome is *nikao* which means "to subdue" (#3528 Strong 1995). Before we deal with what happened, let's bring together the Scriptures which deal with when it happened.

Back in Chapter 7 we examined how the true Church is typed in Scripture as a woman working earth's garden with Christ. We left off with the woman fleeing into the wilderness where she is fed 1260 prophetic days (Revelation 12:6). This started not long after Christ's resurrection mentioned in verse 5. Verses 7-10 reveal that Satan lost a huge battle in heaven, and he and the demons were cast to the earth. Let's quote verses 7-9: "And war broke out in heaven: Michael and his angels fought with the dragon; and the dragon and his angels fought, but they did not prevail, nor was a place found for them in heaven any longer. So the great dragon was cast out, that serpent of old, called the Devil and Satan, who deceives the whole world; he was cast to the earth, and his angels were cast out with him."

Verse 10 goes on to explain that the war would continue on earth with Christ fighting Satan from within His Church, by analogy a woman. In verse 11 we are told of these faithful brethren: "And they overcame him by the blood of the Lamb and by the word of their testimony [*marturia*, "evidence given" (#3141 Strong 1995)], and they did not love their lives to the death."

Because of Christ's victory on the cross, His blood was then made available to expiate sin, making it nearly impossible for Satan to defeat the Church. Unfortunately for Satan and his realm, he had little choice but to continue to wage war with the woman, as we see in verses 13 and 14: "Now when the dragon saw that he had been cast to the earth, he persecuted the woman who gave birth to the male Child [Christ]. But the woman was given two wings of a great eagle, that she might fly into the wilderness to her place, where she is nourished for a time and times and half a time, from the presence of the serpent." Obviously the 1260 prophetic days and the "time and times, and half a time" are speaking of the same thing. They both refer to the woman being nourished in the wilderness and away from the presence of the serpent.

Beyond a doubt Satan is the dragon and the serpent waging spiritual warfare on the woman. The woman is composed of the true followers of Christ, His Church. For 1260 prophetic days she is nourished and protected from the presence of Satan. She is persecuted (verse 13) but not overcome. Both chapter 11 and chapter 12 of Revelation commence with the disciples' commission that took effect at the first Pentecost following Christ's resurrection. That first Pentecost was the precise point in time that the word began to live in them and give them breath.

Revelation 13 also backs up to Christ's death and resurrection but approaches them from a different perspective. Chapter 13 takes the point of view of how Satan makes war on the Church. Whereas it is Christ who speaks the truth through the mouth of the Church, Satan influences a deceived world to accept his lies as the truth and persecutes the true Church for not going along. Satan's power working in people is called a beast, which forms an image of his character. We will pick up the history of this beast by reading the last verse of chapter 12 and then continuing through verse 4 of chapter 13:

"And the dragon was enraged with the woman, and he went to make war with the rest of her offspring, who keep the commandments of God and have the testimony of Jesus Christ. Then I stood on the sand of the sea. And I saw a beast rising up out of the sea, having seven heads and ten horns, and on his horns ten crowns, and on his heads a blasphemous name. Now the beast which I saw was like a leopard, his feet were like the feet of a bear, and his mouth like the mouth of a lion. The dragon gave him his power, his throne, and great authority. And I saw one of his heads as if it had been mortally wounded, and his deadly wound was healed. And all the world marveled and followed the beast. So they worshipped the dragon who gave authority to the beast; and they worshipped the beast, saying, 'Who is like the beast? Who is able to make war with him?'"

This is the same beast power we covered in Chapter 7. In Chapter 7 we compared the image in Nebuchadnezzar's dream (Daniel chapter 2) to the beast in Revelation 17. Those Scriptures clearly show that Satan has fought God by influencing certain nations and peoples to attack God's woman, His Church. He did this in a very physical way in the Old Testament times and has continued to do so both physically and spiritually since Christ's first coming. Satan has always done all he can to stamp out the knowledge of God, His holy days, and His prophetic calendar.

The gospel of John chapter 8 verse 44 calls Satan a liar and the father of lies. Spiritual warfare has predominantly been a battle between God's truth and Satan's lies. Both God and Satan employ the mouths of human beings through which they wage war. The battleground is the hearts and minds of men. We continue now in Revelation 13 verses 5-7: "And he [the beast] was given a mouth speaking great things and blasphemies, and he was given authority to continue for forty-two months. Then he opened his mouth in blasphemy against God, to blaspheme His name, His tabernacle, and those who dwell in heaven. It was granted to him to make war with the saints and to overcome them. And authority was given him over every tribe, tongue, and nation."

Now finally we know what happened to the two witnesses! They were overcome by what came out of Satan's mouth, his breath which was pushed through the vocal chords of those deceived into conveying his horrible thoughts. By these false words he attacked God and His people! By this simple but very effective tactic, God's people, both of the Old Testament and the New Testament, have suffered tremendously. Anyone keeping God's Sabbath and holy days down through time has suffered persecution and tribulation. The fulfillment of God's holy days spells utter defeat for Satan and his tyrannical system of spiritual governance. Therefore he will stop at nothing to stamp out God's truth. He has used holocausts, pogroms, persecutions, and war. But his most sinister weapon is unrepented sin in the lives of God's saints. For Satan, getting a saint to knowingly blaspheme God is the ultimate triumph. A distant second is to get a saint to unknowingly blaspheme God's name. In either case, it is Satan's evil breath uttering his lies through God's very own people. The result is the death of the truth. Scripture reveals that for a very short time at the end of the age both the sun and moon (Christ and His Church) go dark (Matthew 24:29). At that time God the Father who has kept the day and the hour of Christ's return in His own custody and control will say enough is enough. He will then send Christ to liberate the earth from Satan's tyranny at a day and hour that will surprise us all.

The truth is stranger than any fiction. God's plan and thoughts are far deeper than any human being can fathom. To validate what we have just said, it is important to find more Scriptures to back it up. Then we can place the information on God's prophetic calendar of events.

First we go to Daniel 7 verses 19-27: "Then I wished to know the truth about the fourth beast, which was different from all the others, exceedingly dreadful, with its teeth of iron and its nails of bronze, which devoured, broke in pieces, and trampled the residue with its feet; and the ten horns that were on its head, and the other horn which came up, before which three fell, namely, that horn which had eyes and a mouth which spoke pompous words, whose appearance was greater than his fellows. I was watching; and the same horn was making war against the saints, and prevailing against them, until the Ancient of Days came, and a judgment was made in favor of the saints of the Most High, and the time came for the saints to possess the kingdom. Thus he said: 'The fourth beast shall be a fourth kingdom on earth, which shall be different from all other kingdoms, and shall devour the whole earth, trample it and break it in pieces. The ten horns are ten kings who shall arise from this kingdom. And another shall rise after them; he shall be different from the first ones, and shall subdue three kings. He shall speak pompous words against the Most High, shall persecute the saints of the Most High, and shall intend to change times and law. Then the saints shall be given into his hand for a time and times and half a time [42 months or 1260 days]. But the court shall be seated, and they shall take away his dominion, to consume and destroy it forever. Then the kingdom and dominion, and the greatness of the kingdoms under the whole heaven, shall be given to the people, the saints of the Most High. His kingdom is an everlasting kingdom, and all dominions shall serve and obey Him.'" The saints are persecuted, some unto death, for 1260 prophetic days but are not overcome by Satan's lies and deceit. The gospel of the kingdom was not able to be stopped during that period of time.

Satan is the one whose spiritual kingdom is different from any human kingdom, and he is responsible for pushing mankind to hate each other and hate God's people. He will not prevail against God, but will for a short time overcome and overwhelm God's Church in the latter days.

Another sobering Scripture is back in Revelation 13:11-18 which supplies more vital information: "Then I saw another beast coming up out of the earth, and he had two horns like a lamb and spoke like a dragon. And he exercises all the authority of the first beast in his presence, and causes the earth and those who dwell in it to worship the first beast, whose deadly wound was healed. He performs great signs, so that he even makes fire come down from heaven on the earth in the sight of men. And he deceives those who dwell on the earth by those signs which he was granted to do in the sight of the beast, telling those who dwell on the earth to make an image to the beast who was wounded by the sword and lived. He was granted power to give breath to the image of the beast, that the image of the beast should both speak and cause as many as would not worship the image of the beast to be killed. He causes all, both small and great, rich and poor, free and slave, to receive a mark on their right hand or on their foreheads, and that no one may buy or sell except one who has the mark or the name of the beast, or the number of his name. Here is wisdom. Let him who has understanding calculate the number of the beast, for it is the number of a man: His number is 666."

666 - The Antichrist

"He causes all, both small and great, rich and poor, free and slave, to receive a mark on their right hand or on their foreheads, and that no one may buy or sell except one who has the mark or the name of the beast, or the number of his name. Here is wisdom. Let him who has understanding calculate the number of the beast, for it is the number of a man: His number is 666."

These verses have had people pointing fingers at others for a long time. By various means of calculation, Hitler, the Pope, and various political and religious leaders have had this stigma attached to them. Today the most popular theory involves a young man somewhere, full of evil, brilliant of mind, and extremely cunning who is preparing to rule the world. He will use modern technology, like mini-computer chips and credit cards, to control all of the world's commerce during the great tribulation. This evil man will cause the whole earth to worship him as god, and those who refuse will suffer horribly. A torrent of books, movies, television shows, and religious publications have deluged the planet. Not only have their authors, scholars, and directors scared us out of our wits, but they prospered very well financially while doing so. Interestingly, they have had no trouble getting us to buy, sell, and trade in their "wares." The only problem is that none of it is biblical.

The name "Christ" comes from the Greek word Christos meaning the "anointed, i.e. the Messiah" (#5547 Strong 1995). This word derives from chrio (#5548 Strong 1995), to anoint with oil and consecrate to an office or religious service rendering to mankind what is needed. Jesus Christ was Immanuel, or "God with us." Since His death and resurrection, He has dwelt within those Christians to whom have been granted His Holy Spirit.

One can claim to be against Christ, that is antichrist, but no human being can claim to be the Antichrist. Antichrist means the opposite of Christ. Christ came to ultimately replace the god of this world, Satan. Satan has ruled this world for six thousand years, and he can enter people as he did with Judas (Luke 22:3), who betrayed Christ. Satan is the only being who has ever held the titles of god and ruler of this world. In Ezekiel 28:14, Lucifer was called the anointed cherub, meaning the one with outstretched wings who has been anointed with oil or consecrated. Isaiah 14:12-16 speaks of the fallen Lucifer as "the man." In Scripture, angels are often depicted as beings that look like men and sometimes are even called men. (See the angel Gabriel referred to as the man in Daniel 9:21.)

The number of the beast and Antichrist is 666, for he has fallen short of God in every way since he fell from his position in heaven. God's number is 7, sheba in Hebrew, the cardinal number "seven (as the sacred full one)… seven times; by implication a week" (#7651 Strong 1995). That makes sense, for God rested on the seventh day at creation when He saw that all He had made was good. The last day of every week is God's Sabbath. The seventh Millennium is God's. Satan rules for the first 6000 years, depicted by the first six days each week. Therefore 666 (#5516 Strong 1995) is the number of his name, with the last "6" actually coming from the Greek word stigma (#4742 Strong 1995). As Satan has deceived the whole world (Revelation 12:9), the whole world has been stigmatized by his influence and attitudes, for all of us have sinned. We have been buying, selling, and trading in his merchandize. Christ wants us to put on His mark and be more like Him, growing in perfection, trading in forgiveness of debt, so that we can be forgiven. "Our Father in heaven, hallowed be Your name. Your kingdom come. Your will be done on earth as it is in heaven. Give us this day our daily bread. And forgive us our debts, as we forgive our debtors…For if you forgive men their trespasses, your heavenly Father will also forgive you" (Matthew 6:9-12, 14).

Here we can see a second beast that rises out of the earth that looks like a lamb but speaks like a dragon. Christ is called the Lamb of God (John 1:29, 36), and His Church is composed of sheep. Satan is a dragon, as we saw in Revelation 12. When God's people are overcome at the end of the age, it is because they have been deceived into speaking Satan's lies, giving it the voice of a dragon. The lie is composed of three parts:

 1. God seeks to destroy most of mankind at the end of the age in a terrifying fit of rage and vengeance.

 2. False prophecies and heresy bolstered by false signs and lying wonders.

 3. Change times, seasons, and laws by coaxing mankind into observing Satan's counterfeit agenda and holy days, showing himself to be equal to God the Father and Jesus Christ.

 It is a fair question to ask how this could possibly happen. The answer is contained in the Scriptures we just read. The two witnesses successfully lived in the Church for 1260 prophetic days, using the body of Christ to preach the good news of the gospel of the kingdom, cast out demons, and heal the sick. After those days were completed, Satan morphed the Church into an image of himself by overcoming it from within. As a matter of fact, Revelation 13:14-15 actually said as much if we have ears to hear. Let's read them once again, putting in one correction supported by most of the original Biblical texts:

 "And he [Satan, the dragon] deceives those who dwell on the earth by those signs which he was granted to do in the sight of the beast, telling those who dwell on the earth to make an image to the beast who was wounded by the sword and lived. He was granted power to give breath to the image of the beast, that the image of the beast should both speak and cause as many as would not worship the image of the beast to be killed." The phrase, "those who dwell on the earth" is translated differently in the majority of the old Greek texts, having been changed in the last 150 years by scholars thinking they were making the Scripture clearer. (See the Preface to the New King James Version of the Bible, Thomas Nelson Inc.) The majority of old texts render "those who dwell on the earth" as "My own people who dwell on the earth." This is much more consistent with the idea of a lamb that speaks like a dragon. Additionally, verse 15 told us that power and breath were given to the image to speak on Satan's behalf! It is clear that at the very end of the age Satan corrupts what Christ did on that first Pentecost. That is when Christ gave His disciples power and breath, thus making the two witnesses come alive in them. This incredible turn of events is actually well documented in other Scriptures and is easily placed on God's prophetic calendar. It is verifiably the most horrible event the New Testament Church has had to endure, but due to a former physical fulfillment, it can be understood by those with ears to hear.

In Chapter 2 we took a calm look at the end of the world. In that chapter (review it now if you need to, as it was very brief), Christ responded to His disciples' questions about the signs of Christ's second coming and the end of the age (Matthew 24:3). Christ used the next few verses to warn them what signs would be spoken in His name to deceive His followers down through time. This would be especially true at the end of the age. Christ listed these false signs in verses 6 and 7: "And you will hear of wars and rumors of wars. See that you are not troubled; for all these things must come to pass, but the end is not yet. For nation will rise against nation, and kingdom against kingdom. And there will be famines, pestilences, and earthquakes in various places."

In Matthew 24:14 Christ gave us the key physical event that would mark that the end was near: "And this gospel of the kingdom will be preached in all the world as a witness to all the nations, and then the end will come." In other words, when the great commission had gone to the whole world (fulfilling what Christ said in Acts 1 verse 8: "But you shall receive power when the Holy Spirit has come upon you; and you shall be witnesses to Me in Jerusalem, and in all Judea and Samaria, and to the end of the earth"), only then could the end-time sequence of events begin to unfold. The gospel of the kingdom could not have been preached to the whole world until the technological advances of the Twentieth Century. The advent of television, radio, and huge printing presses made fulfillment of the great commission possible.

We can now cross reference Revelation 11:1-7 and Revelation 13 with Acts 1:8 and Matthew 24:14. This allows us to see how the work of the two witnesses was accomplished and what the next prophetic event would follow. Christ gave the answer in Matthew 24:15 as He continued telling His disciples the signs that would accompany His return: "Therefore when you see the 'abomination of desolation,' spoken of by Daniel the prophet, standing in the holy place (whoever reads, let him understand) then let those who are in Judea flee to the mountains." We must now turn back to the prophet Daniel to glean more information.

Daniel was given a long prophecy which began in his day and reached all the way to the present. The prophecy began in chapter 10 and continued through chapter 11 and concluded in chapter 12. Chapter 12 verses 1-3 open with the final stages of the long war between good and evil, God and Satan: "At that time Michael [the great angel] shall stand up, the great prince who stands watch over the sons of your people; and there shall be a time of trouble, such as never was since there was a nation, even to that time. And at that time, your people shall be delivered, every one who is found written in the book. And many of those who sleep in the dust of the earth shall awake, some to everlasting life, some to shame and everlasting contempt. Those who are wise shall shine like the brightness of the firmament, and those who turn many to righteousness like the stars forever and ever." These Scriptures obviously refer to a difficult time followed by Christ's return and the resurrection.

This time of great trouble is unlike any war or trouble that ever came before. That is because it is a spiritual defeat for God's people. Daniel 11:31-33 mentions that it begins with the abomination of desolation. Before we quote these Scriptures, you need to know this is a dual prophecy with the first fulfillment occurring in 586 B.C. We will look into that a little later, as we are now focusing on our time. "And forces shall be mustered by him, and they shall defile the sanctuary fortress; then they shall take away the daily sacrifices [Hebrew *tamiyd* "constant... the regular (daily) sacrifice" #8548 Strong 1995], and place there the abomination of desolation. Those who do wickedly against the covenant he shall corrupt with flattery; but the people who know their God shall be strong, and carry out great exploits. And those of the people who understand shall instruct many; yet for many days they shall fall by sword and flame, by captivity and plundering."

When Daniel penned these words, one Old Testament fulfillment had taken place in 586 B.C. That was the destruction of Jerusalem and Solomon's temple. This was the original abomination of desolation. Babylon under Nebuchadnezzar had abominated the temple and desolated the city. A second Old Testament fulfillment took place in 167 B.C. when Antiochus Epiphanes desecrated the temple. (Space does not permit covering these in detail.) Daniel did not know that there would be two fulfillments that the New Testament Church would experience. He honestly did not even know a New Testament would be written someday.

Near the beginning of the New Testament experience Rome surrounded Jerusalem, killed many Jews, and destroyed the temple. General Titus of Rome destroyed Jerusalem, and abominated and desolated the temple in 70 A.D. He did this to the very temple in which Jesus Christ had taught some forty years earlier. Christ Himself prophesied this in Matthew 24:2. "Do you not see all these things? Assuredly, I say to you, not one stone shall be left here upon another, that shall not be thrown down." Christ was prophesying the *last physical* abomination of desolation. It was these very comments that prompted the disciples to ask their now-famous questions about Christ's return and the end of the age. After listing the false signs that He knew would someday be used to deceive His Church, He pointed to one more abomination of desolation. Christ was warning His apostles of a desolation that they would live to see and another to occur in the Church nearly two thousand years later. This one would require wisdom to comprehend, for it would be an all-out spiritual assault on the Church. This final abomination of desolation would not take place until after the gospel of the kingdom had been preached to all the world as a witness. Daniel 12:4-13 holds more pieces of this spiritual puzzle that we need in order to accurately place this spiritual event on God's prophetic calendar.

Remember in Daniel 12:1-3, Daniel was shown a unique time of trouble for God's people just before the resurrection of the saints which accompanies Christ's second coming. We break into a discussion between Daniel and the angelic messenger that is full of information pertinent to the time in which we live. "'But you, Daniel, shut up the words, and seal the book until the time of the end; many shall run to and fro, and knowledge shall increase' [certainly an accurate description of our time]. Then I, Daniel, looked; and there stood two others, one on this riverbank and the other on that riverbank. And one said to the man clothed in linen, who was above the waters of the river, 'How long shall the fulfillment of these wonders be?' Then I heard the man clothed in linen, who was above the waters of the river, when he held up his right hand and his left hand to heaven, and swore by Him who lives forever, that it shall be for a time, times, and half a time [dividing of time, in this case]; and when the power of the holy people has been completely shattered, all these things shall be finished [shattering the power to fight Satan with the two witnesses]. Although I heard, I did not understand. Then I said, 'My lord, what shall be the end of these things?' And he said, 'Go your way, Daniel, for the words are closed up and sealed till the time of the end. Many shall be purified, made white, and refined, but the wicked shall do wickedly; and none of the wicked shall understand, but the wise shall understand. And from the time that the daily sacrifice is taken away, and the abomination of desolation is set up, there shall be one thousand two hundred and ninety days. Blessed is he who waits, and comes to the one thousand three hundred and thirty-five days. But you, go your way till the end; for you shall rest, and will arise to your inheritance at the end of the days.'" This remarkable prophecy is dual in nature, with a former and later fulfillment. For that reason it is best to get all the scriptural evidence laid out side by side as on Table 3, so we can visualize things.

Scripture	Prophetic Time Length	Basic Description
Revelation 12:6	1260 days	Woman hidden and fed in wilderness
Revelation 12:14	Time, times, half a time: 1260 days	Woman hidden and fed in wilderness
Revelation 13:5	42 months	1260 prophetic days of persecution on those bearing witness
Revelation 11:2	42 months	Outer court trampled by Gentiles, which is area outside the spiritual temple
Revelation 11:3	1260 days	Length of time two witnesses speak truth through God's Church, the woman
	All the above are the same length of prophetic time.	Length of time gospel is preached before it reaches the entire world
Daniel 12:11	1290 days	Abomination of desolation takes place 30 prophetic days after two witnesses finish prophesying. Coincides with collapse of two witnesses.
Daniel 12:12	1335 days	Blessing of resurrection as promised to Daniel at end of the days.
Daniel 12:7	Time, times, half a time	

Table 3

There are probably thousands of dual fulfillments hidden within the pages of the Old and New Testaments. It is a richly rewarding exercise to mine the Scriptures and study them. The stated goal of this book is to relieve the fear and anxiety caused by erroneous beliefs regarding the end of the world, and to help humanity prepare for and embrace the wonderful time and season we are about to enter. We have to be careful not to branch off in too many directions, for time, space, and clarity do not allow for it, however, the words of God are so interesting it is hard not to.

The main theme of the entire Bible is the war between God and Satan, a war between good and evil. God is not at war with the human race. God wants to deliver humanity from tyranny, injustice, and ignorance. The gospel of the kingdom is the good news that God intends to set us free. God's holy days are the step-by-step plan

He is following to accomplish this.

Sticking to this approach, we now introduce Figure 14. This graphic brings together what we have learned about the seasons, God's holy days, and the prophetic days of Daniel 12 and Revelation 11, 12, and 13. By comparing Figures 11 through 13, you will notice that the circle representing the New Testament Church has been "slid" back or superimposed over the Old Testament circle to show how the seasons progress naturally. When the Old Testament congregation reaches fall, the New Testament Church enters spring. Creation portrays this in its annual rhythms. When the Northern Hemisphere enters fall, the Southern Hemisphere enters spring with the equator dividing the seasons in half. Thus we can see how every annual cycle of the seasons portrays God's concept of duality with a former and a latter fulfillment, each equal to one-half of the whole. If you look at the concentric circles carefully with a little imagination, you can see phases of the moon. We have already established in Scripture that the moon represents the Church, and its monthly cycle determines when to keep the holy days. In Satan's war against God he tried unsuccessfully to put out the light of the sun permanently by killing Christ, and he has been trying ever since that first Pentecost to make the moon grow dark. He briefly succeeds very near the end of the age, but the war is not over until it's over, as it is sometimes said.

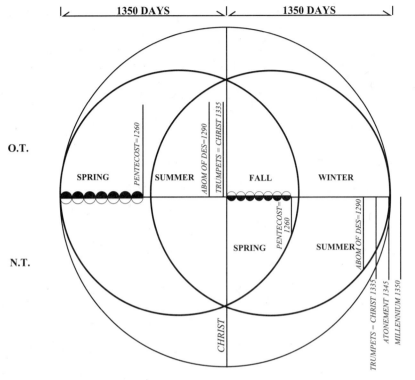

1350 DAYS | 1350 DAYS

O.T.

PENTECOST=1260

ABOM OF DES=1290

TRUMPETS = CHRIST 1335

SPRING   SUMMER   FALL   WINTER

SPRING   SUMMER

N.T.

PENTECOST= 1260

ABOM OF DES=1290

TRUMPETS = CHRIST 1335

ATONEMENT 1345

MILLENNIUM 1350

CHRIST

Figure 14

Thy Kingdom Come

Christ came preaching the gospel of the kingdom, and His great commission to the Church was to keep the message spreading until it reached the ends of the earth. He told the crowds that followed Him that they were near the kingdom of God whenever they were in His presence. One had to accept His statements on faith because when looking at Him, one saw nothing remarkable. He did not stand out in a crowd (John 8:59). He was not wealthy. He was not born to a high station in life, being a carpenter and the son of a carpenter.

In Luke 17:20-21 He said that we cannot see the coming kingdom by physical eyesight: "Now when He was asked by the Pharisees [some of the religious leaders of the time] when the kingdom of God would come, He answered them and said, 'The kingdom of God does not come with observation; nor will they say, "See here!" or "See there!" for indeed, the kingdom of God is within you."" "Within you" is better translated "in your midst" (See marginal reference, New King James Version of the Bible, Thomas Nelson, Inc.). The physical eye did not see a king, but every day the crowds witnessed and experienced what it was like to come into contact with the kingdom of God. The blind were given their sight (Mark 8:22-26, Mark 10:46-52). He healed the sick (Matthew 8:8-16). Sinners were forgiven (Matthew 9:1-8), and He freed people from demons (Mark 5:1-13). Just the effects of contact with the king of an unseeable kingdom brought relief from pain, healing, freedom from evil, and lifting of the burdens of guilt. Touching this tiny kingdom surrounding one Man was to experience mercy, kindness, compassion, and power that could be found nowhere else on earth!

In the synagogue on one particular Sabbath day, Christ was given an opportunity to read Scripture. He chose to read a prophecy about Himself in the Book of Isaiah. Luke 4 verses 18-19: "The Spirit of the Lord is upon Me, because He has anointed Me to preach the gospel to the poor; He has sent Me to heal the broken hearted, to proclaim liberty to the captives and recovery of sight to the blind, to set at liberty those who are oppressed; to proclaim the acceptable year of the Lord." The gospel of the kingdom means to proclaim the good news that God is establishing it one step at a time by fulfilling the promises embodied in the holy days. The next event on the schedule is the return of Jesus Christ, pictured by the holy day called the Feast of Trumpets. At that time the whole earth will come into contact with the kingdom of God. The world will begin experiencing peace, healing, and liberty on an unprecedented scale.

Why are people afraid to be liberated, to be set free from tyranny, disease, war, and famine? Because Satan, who deceives the whole world (Revelation 12:9), has covered the world with lies. He has convinced virtually the whole world, including Christendom, to believe that it is God's intention to punish the human race with unspeakable horrors at the end of the world.

Satan has gotten many to believe that it is God the Father

and Jesus Christ behind the creation of nuclear weapons, energy shortages, financial collapse, droughts, famines, and disease. Behind these sorrows are Satan and the four horsemen of the Apocalypse. It is Christ who will soon set us free as the greatest Liberator of all time. With proper understanding of God's word, His holy days, and where we are in His times and seasons, the fears and burdens induced by ignorance can now be lifted. As fog is burned off by the sun and blown away by wind, so shall God's truth remove the evil influences that hold us captive. The darkness causes interminable strife, divides people and nations, fosters greed, corruption, and injustice. The influence behind tyrants and oppressors is coming to a swift end.

The gospel of the kingdom did reach the entire world as a witness during the Twentieth Century. The Twentieth Century saw a small Sabbath-keeping Church re-embrace God's holy days and powerfully preach the gospel of the kingdom to the world. Over the air waves, on television, through printed word, and personal evangelism a small Church stood behind the lone figure of Herbert W. Armstrong to proclaim the gospel of the kingdom and marvelous hope just ahead. This is when Matthew 24:14 fulfilled the great commission given to the disciples on that first Pentecost. Here is an excerpt from *The Plain Truth* (June-July 1981 issue), the flagship publication of what was then known as the Worldwide Church of God. The article was entitled "Blood, Sweat and Tears".

"This is a 'blood, sweat, and tears' talk with our readers - with apologies to the late Sir Winston Churchill. At Britain's darkest hour of World War II, Prime Minister Churchill's 'blood, sweat, and tears' speech saved the nation.

"It struck through to the hearts of the British people. It moved their emotions. Like an electric shock it gave them hope. It stirred their determination, aroused a willingness to suffer any sacrifice or privation, that their country might survive.

"Today, as surely as Britain faced the question of survival then, all humanity faces the question of SURVIVAL now - the survival of the human race!

"We don't like to think about it. We shrink from facing up to the existing facts. I know that well! But there is a story to be told about that, and I propose to tell it now.

"Forty-seven years ago a tiny handful of financially poor but sober people did face up to it. They volunteered to join me in a 'blood, sweat, and tears' sacrifice to do something about it. As time went on, others caught the vision, volunteered to join with them. Now, in humanity's darkest hour - with most of humanity lethargically refusing to face up to it - our deliverance is near. Glorious victory is in sight; humanity will be saved alive. The peaceful, happy, prosperous, joyful WORLD TOMORROW is soon to dawn.

"The world little realizes now, but soon it will come to astonished awareness of the fact that these volunteers have had something vital to do with it.

"Their unselfish sacrifice has gone too long unnoticed. I feel it is high time that I give acknowledgement, and pay full tribute to those to whom tribute is due. They have made possible a very remarkable thing - something never done before! It is something that concerns every reader of this magazine.

"This magazine now has a vast readership of several million people. Before this vast audience I want to give public recognition of the loving service, often at great personal sacrifice, given by a comparatively small army of volunteers. They have made it possible for YOU to hold this fine-quality magazine in your hands just now. They have also done far more.

"These are the loyal co-workers who have made possible *The World Tomorrow* broadcast."

The extent to which the gospel of the kingdom reached the whole world as a witness is evidenced by the many influential people and world leaders who expressed condolences upon Mr. Armstrong's death in January 1986.

The following is quoted from *The Worldwide News* of February 10, 1986. "These tributes only begin to cover the many facets of Mr. Armstrong's life and work. Much more could have been written, but space did not permit..."

"I was greatly saddened to learn of the passing away of Mr. Armstrong. From the time of the San Francisco [Calif.] Conference which he attended as a journalist, Mr. Armstrong took a strong and supporting interest in the United Nations. With his wide ties throughout the world, he pursued the cause of peace and harmony among all peoples. My wife and I indeed recall our meeting with him in San Francisco last June and had looked forward to seeing him subsequently in New York. We would like to express our sincere condolences on this sad occasion. Javier Perez de Cuellar, Secretary-General United Nations."

"To the congregation, Worldwide Church of God: Nancy and I join all those mourning the loss of Herbert W. Armstrong. As founder and leader of the Worldwide Church of God, Mr. Armstrong contributed to sharing the word of the Lord with his community and with people throughout the nation. You can take pride in his legacy. Our prayers are with you. God bless you. Ronald and Nancy Reagan, President of the United States"

"I feel that loss in a very special way...This morning my thoughts flash back over the years in which I watch from afar the development of your beautiful campus. Little did I dream that years later, although I was not a member of the Church, I was to share so generously in Mr. Armstrong's unselfish and dedicated support of our community, its supporting organizations and in the furtherance of its cultural growth. I can scarcely name an activity in which Ambassador has not in some way been involved! The full measure of your loss can only be appreciated by your Church Family, I know. But his loss will be felt by so many outside the church who so much admired and appreciated his splendid concern for his community. Myron G. Stolp, Rotary International, Pasadena"

"We learned with deep sorrow of the passing away of Mr. Herbert W. Armstrong, leader of the Worldwide Church of God. Please convey to his family and to the members of your church our sympathies and condolences. Mr. Armstrong will be remembered as a great spiritual leader and a true friend of Israel. Jacob Even, Consul General of Israel, Los Angeles"

"Their majesties instructed me to convey their heartfelt sympathies and condolences on the passing away of Mr. Herbert W. Armstrong and their hope that the life of benevolence, altruism and the drive for better understanding among peoples which Mr. Armstrong led will continue to be the inspirational path for others to follow. Adnan Abu Odeh, Minister, Royal Hashemite Court"

"I was saddened to learn of the death of our good friend Herbert Armstrong. It has been a great shock to members of my family and I am sure also to the numerous friends he had in Jordan. He was truly a great man of vision and his campaign for understanding and co-existence are very much valued. I am confident that his colleagues will carry on with his mission and his great work. Mohammed Kamal, Jordanian Ambassador to the United States"

"The queen and I have learnt with deep sorrow and profound sadness at the news of the passing away of Mr. Herbert W. Armstrong, the founder and chairman of Ambassador Foundation who, through his understanding, wisdom and humanitarianism, has sought to give encouragement and assistance to people all over the world, particularly to Thailand where he has devoted much of his time and resources, thereby becoming a close and valuable friend of our country. We hasten to express to the members of Mr. Armstrong's family, his colleagues at the Ambassador Foundation and Ambassador College our sincere sympathy and heartfelt condolences for this sad and irreparable loss, which will be felt not only in the United States of America but also in Thailand. Bhumibol Adulyadej, King of Thailand"

"Members of the Royal Thai Embassy's staff join me in sending our deepest sympathy and heartfelt condolences to the Armstrong family on the passing away of Mr. Herbert Armstrong, a great friend of Thailand and a truly fine human being. It was a privilege to have known and worked with Mr. Armstrong and we will always be thankful for the fine efforts and contributions that Mr. Armstrong has made to the betterment of understanding and friendship between the peoples of Thailand and the United States. Kasem S. Kasemsri, Ambassador, Thai Embassy, Washington,

D.C."

"We are aware of the vital contribution which President Armstrong made for world peace. And his benevolent love shown to our people and our country is always in our heart. Moreover, his generous aid to our Tel Zeror Archaeological Project in Israel through your Foundation will long be remembered by us all. We extend our deepest sympathies and heartfelt condolences to you and to all whom President Armstrong loved in this world. Koichiro Ishikawa, Tel Zeror Archaeological Project"

"The royal Nepalese Embassy wishes to transmit the following message of condolence from their Majesties the King and Queen of Nepal to the Ambassador Foundation: The Queen and I are grieved to hear of the sad demise of Herbert Armstrong. He was a man truly dedicated to the cause of serving humanity. May his soul rest in peace. Birendra Bir Bikram Shah Dev, King of Nepal"

"Grieved and shocked to learn the passing away of Mr. Herbert Armstrong, chairman of Ambassador Foundation, a good friend to the Chinese people. His contribution to mutual understanding and friendship between the peoples of China and the United States will remain forever in our hearts. Please convey my condolences to his family and relatives. Tang Shubei, Consul General of China, San Francisco"

"Heartfelt condolences and deepest sympathies on passing away of Mr. Herbert W. Armstrong and founder president of Ambassador Foundation. Irreplaceable loss for the world at large. His message of peace and humanitarianism will glow forever. May he rest in peace. Festus Perera, Minister of Fisheries, Sri Lanka"

"Our deepest sympathies on the death of Dr. Herbert W. Armstrong, founder-president of Ambassador Foundation. Grateful for services rendered by him to Sri Lanka and for carrying the message of peace throughout the world. May he rest in peace. G. M. Premachandra, Deputy Minister of Fisheries, Sri Lanka"

It has taken nearly two thousand long and difficult years for a small Church hidden in the wilderness of religious confusion to finally take the gospel of the kingdom to the entire world as a witness.

The spring season of 1260 prophetic days took approximately 1950 years before progress and technological advances made it all possible. The words spoken to Daniel in chapter 12 verse 4 had finally been realized: "But you, Daniel, shut up the words, and seal the book until the time of the end; many shall run to and fro, and knowledge shall increase."

The truth of the gospel was a lit torch faithfully passed from Church generation to Church generation. Much like a candle flame touching the wick of the next candle, the truth was kept alive. But just as the moon above waxes to full brightness and then wanes, so has the brightness of the Church. The abomination and desolation of God's spiritual temple and city (Hebrews 12:18-24) temporarily put a bushel basket over that light and threatened to permanently snuff out the wicks of those who carried it. Before it can be explained how this came to be, we need to quote enough Scripture so we can have absolute certainty that God wins in the end; this means victory for the human race as well. Think of God doing spiritually what we would do physically to coax a dying ember back to life – gently breathing on it, and, as the spark comes to life, blowing on it harder until the lamp or candle burns brightly. Now listen to God's voice. Matthew 12 verses 18-21: "Behold! My Servant whom I have chosen, My Beloved in whom My soul is well pleased! I will put My Spirit upon Him, and He will declare justice to the Gentiles. He will not quarrel nor cry out, nor will anyone hear His voice in the streets. A bruised reed He will not break, and smoking flax He will not quench, till He sends forth justice to victory; and in His name Gentiles will trust."

Smoking flax is a lamp wick. These verses were taken from Isaiah 42:3, but to grasp the full effect of how Christ works through the Church, let's also read Isaiah 42 verses 1-9: "'Behold! My Servant whom I uphold, My Elect One in whom My soul delights! I have put My Spirit upon Him; He will bring forth justice to the Gentiles. He will not cry out, nor raise His voice, nor cause His voice to be heard in the street. A bruised reed He will not break, and smoking flax He will not quench; He will bring forth justice for truth. He will not fail nor be discouraged, till He has established justice in the earth; and the coastlands shall wait for His law.' Thus says God the Lord, who created the heavens and stretched them out, who spread forth the earth and that which comes from it, who gives breath to the people on it, and spirit to those who walk on it: 'I, the Lord, have called You in righteousness, and will hold Your hand; I will keep You and give You as a covenant to the people, as a light to the Gentiles, to open blind eyes, to bring out prisoners from the prison, those who sit in darkness from the prison house. I am the Lord, that is My name; and My glory I will not give to another, nor My praise to carved images. Behold, the former things have come to pass, and new things I declare; before they spring forth I tell you of them.'"

Matthew 5 verses 13-16: "You are the salt of the earth; but if the salt loses its flavor, how shall it be seasoned? It is then good for nothing but to be thrown out and trampled underfoot by men. You are the light of the world. A city that is set on a hill cannot be hidden. Nor do they light a lamp and put it under a basket, but on a lampstand, and it gives light to all who are in the house. Let your light so shine before men, that they may see your good works and glorify your Father in heaven."

Now it is easier to see why those carrying the breath of God's word within them are not buried when they are overcome and die in Revelation 11:7. It is the lamp of the two witnesses that goes out for three and one-half prophetic days. It only requires the breath of life to blow on them once again, a form of spiritual resuscitation, to get them on their feet. Read of this in verses 7-11 and notice how the joy of Satan's demons on the earth quickly changes to fear: "When they finished their testimony, the beast that ascends out of the bottomless pit will make war against them, overcome them, and kill them. And their dead bodies will lie in the street of the great city which spiritually is called Sodom and Egypt, where also our Lord was crucified. Then those from the peoples, tribes, tongues, and nations will see their dead bodies three-and-a-half days, and not allow their dead bodies to be put into graves. And those who dwell on the earth will rejoice over them, make merry, and send gifts to one another, because these two prophets tormented those who dwell on the earth. Now after the three-and-a-half days the breath of life from God entered them, and they stood on their feet, and great fear fell on those who saw them."

The next verse (12) gives us a key reference point so that we can place this event on God's calendar of events. Clearly, verse 11 shows us the resurrection that takes place on the 1335th prophetic day: "And they heard a loud voice from heaven saying to them, 'Come up here.' And they ascended to heaven in a cloud, and their enemies saw them." This marks the end of the war for the firstfruits.

Some who had the opportunity to be firstfruits fell short of the mark and are left behind on earth. For them, being left behind is a very sad time, called a woe in verse 14. This squares with the prophecy in Daniel 12 verses 2-3: "And many of those who sleep in the dust of the earth shall awake, some to everlasting life, some to shame and everlasting contempt. Those who are wise shall shine like the brightness of the firmament, and those who turn many to righteousness like the stars forever and ever." Notice that it is the wise who shine. The same word is used in verse 10 that says the wise (*sakal* in Hebrew "circumspect and hence, intelligent" - #7919 Strong 1995) will understand, spiritually speaking.

Now we will cross reference this event with the famous parable of the ten virgins in Matthew 25 verses 1-13: "Then the kingdom of heaven shall be likened to ten virgins who took their lamps and went out to meet the bridegroom. Now five of them were wise, and five were foolish. Those who were foolish took their lamps and took no oil with them, but the wise took oil in their vessels with their lamps. But while the bridegroom was delayed, they all slumbered and slept. And at midnight a cry was heard: 'Behold, the bridegroom is coming; go out to meet him!' Then all those virgins arose and trimmed their lamps. And the foolish said to the wise, 'Give us some of your oil, for our lamps are going out.' But the wise answered, saying, 'No, lest there should not be enough for us and you; but go rather to those who sell, and buy for yourselves.' And while they went to buy, the bridegroom came, and those who were ready went in with him to the wedding; and the door was shut. Afterward the other virgins came also, saying,

'Lord, Lord, open to us!' But he answered and said, 'Assuredly, I say to you, I do not know you.' Watch therefore, for you know neither the day nor the hour in which the Son of Man is coming."

This parable definitely speaks about Christ's return and how His servants project the light of God's word. Believing is not enough, for "faith without works is dead" (James 2:20). (See also James 1:21-27.) Christ often said a believer must "take up his cross, and follow Me." The obvious exhortation is to become like Him, full of love, mercy, and outgoing concern for others. In the Greek this was an expression which meant to extinguish all selfishness (#4717 Strong 1995).

Therefore, even if a person was called and baptized, they could still fall far short of building the character and attributes of Christ and find themselves "left behind" at the resurrection. This explains why after the resurrection of the witnesses in Revelation 11 there is a remnant left behind, and to them this becomes a woeful time. Let's read in Revelation 11:13-14 followed by Matthew 24 verses 36-44: "In the same hour there was a great earthquake, and a tenth of the city fell. In the earthquake seven thousand people were killed, and the rest were afraid and gave glory to the God of heaven. The second woe is past. Behold, the third woe is coming quickly." "But of that day and hour no one knows, not even the angels of heaven, but My Father only. But as the days of Noah were, so also will the coming of the Son of Man be. For as in the days before the flood, they were eating and drinking, marrying and giving in marriage, until the day that Noah entered the ark, and did not know until the flood came and took them all away, so also will the coming of the Son of Man be. Then two men will be in the field: one will be taken and the other left. Two women will be grinding at the mill: one will be taken and the other left. Watch therefore, for you do not know what hour your Lord is coming. But know this, that if the master of the house had known what hour the thief would come, he would have watched and not allowed his house to be broken into. Therefore you also be ready, for the Son of Man is coming at an hour you do not expect."

Please set aside all notion of being left behind on a world gone mad, bent on evil and self-destruction. Nothing could be further from the truth. In the next chapter we will discuss the tribulation and Armageddon, using God's word to learn all about them.

Before we finish this chapter we need to examine the former fulfillment of the fall and resurrection of the two witnesses. The parallel is the death and resurrection of Christ. Note the similarities as we read Matthew 27 verses 45-54: "Now from the sixth hour until the ninth hour there was darkness over all the land. And about the ninth hour Jesus cried out with a loud voice, saying, 'Eli, Eli, lama sabachthani?' that is, 'My God, My God, why have You forsaken Me?' Some of those who stood there, when they heard that, said, 'This Man is calling for Elijah!' Immediately one of them ran and took a sponge, filled it with sour wine and put it on a reed, and offered it to Him to drink. The rest said, 'Let Him alone; let us see if Elijah will come to save Him.' And Jesus cried out again with a loud voice, and yielded up His spirit. Then, behold, the veil of the temple was torn in two from top to bottom; and the earth quaked, and the rocks were split, and the graves were opened; and many bodies of the saints who had fallen asleep were raised; and coming out of the graves after His resurrection, they went into the holy city and appeared to many. So when the centurion and those with him, who were guarding Jesus, saw the earthquake and the things that had happened, they feared greatly, saying, 'Truly this was the Son of God!'"

When Christ breathed His last and gave up His spirit, the sun went dark, the earth quaked, and He was in the grave three days and three nights. All of these are a very close match to what happened to the two witnesses. That is because Christ Himself is the breath of both witnesses, the Old Testament and New Testament. It is His breath that gives the word life and power in those to whom is granted the Holy Spirit. When Christ died, it was the death of the first witness, the Old Testament, because the words comprising it were His. It was by His breath that it was spoken and written through the prophets whom He used. This was to a very small number of

130

people in the congregation of Israel. They had the Holy Spirit and were called to do a work of sacrifice in furthering God's plan. They kept the Sabbath, kept the holy days, taught the people God's ways, and encouraged them to keep the covenant. Now reread verses 51 through 53 of Matthew 27 to see something absolutely astonishing: "Then, behold, the veil of the temple was torn in two from top to bottom; and the earth quaked, and the rocks were split, and the *graves were opened*; and *many bodies of the saints who had fallen asleep were raised; and coming out of the graves after His resurrection*, they went into the holy city and appeared to many. So when the centurion and those with him, who were guarding Jesus, saw the earthquake and the things that had happened, they feared greatly, saying, 'Truly this was the Son of God!'" (emphasis added)

Who were these resurrected saints that came out of their graves after Christ's resurrection? They cannot be the disciples or other Christians, for the Christian Church had not even begun yet, nor had any disciples died. These had to be the prophets who carried the first witness within them as Christ's breathed word! They walked about the city and were seen by many. Abraham, Isaac, Jacob, Isaiah, Daniel, Moses, and others could be seen and spoken to! What do you think would have been the main topic of conversation? Of course they would have spoken about Christ's resurrection and how His life and death fulfilled the prophecies they had spoken and written about. These were the ones spoken of in Hebrews 11 as the faithful martyrs of the past. We quote a few verses from Hebrews 11, the Faith Chapter. Verses 1-3: "Now faith is the substance of things hoped for, the evidence of things not seen. For by it elders obtained a good testimony. By faith we understand that the worlds were framed by the word of God, so that the things which are seen were not made of things which are visible." Verse 13: "These all died in faith, not having received the promises, but having seen them afar off were assured of them, embraced them and confessed that they were strangers and pilgrims on the earth." Verse 16: "But now they desire a better, that is, a heavenly country. Therefore God is not ashamed to be called their God, for He has prepared a city for them."

Verse 28: "By faith he kept the Passover and the sprinkling of blood, lest he who destroyed the firstborn should touch them." (They kept all holy days, including the Sabbath.) Verses 37-40: "They were stoned, they were sawn in two, were tempted, were slain with the sword. They wandered about in sheepskins and goatskins, being destitute, afflicted, tormented – of whom the world was not worthy. They wandered in deserts and mountains, in dens and caves of the earth. And all these, having obtained a good testimony through faith, did not receive the promise, God having provided something better for us, that they should not be made perfect apart from us."

These saints were raised from the dead hoping for the promised rewards as Daniel had been promised in Daniel 12 verses 12-13: "Blessed is he who waits, and comes to the one thousand three hundred and thirty-five days. But you, go your way till the end; for you shall rest, and will arise to your inheritance at the end of the days." Before they could receive eternal life and their entire reward, there was more work to be done. More saints had to be called so the gospel of the kingdom could go to the entire world as a witness in a second fulfillment of prophecy. Another 1260 prophetic days had to elapse and a second 1335th day attained .

We now turn to Revelation 6:9-11 for insight on this truly remarkable incident. "When He opened the fifth seal, I saw under the altar the souls of those who had been slain for the word of God and for the testimony which they held. And they cried with a loud voice, saying, 'How long, O Lord, holy and true, until You judge and avenge our blood on those who dwell on the earth?' Then a white robe was given to each of them; and it was said to them that they should rest a little while longer, until both the number of their fellow servants and their brethren, who would be killed as they were, was completed."

We now know when the fifth seal was opened by Christ. All that could be given to these once dead and now physically alive saints was the blood of Christ to remove their sins, making their garments white. The war would have to continue as the woman worked to produce more saints to fill the spiritual temple with the rest of the firstfruits. In other words, the firstfruits of the 1260 day prophetic period of Pentecost in the Old Testament would have to be joined with the firstfruits of the corresponding 1260 day period of the Christian era.

We close this chapter with Figure 15, which is Figure 14 with the additional symbol of each group of saints. They are pictured by the seven-candled menorah of the Old Testament saints and the seven candlesticks of the New Testament saints. These represent the lamps of God's word that each carried in a dark world.

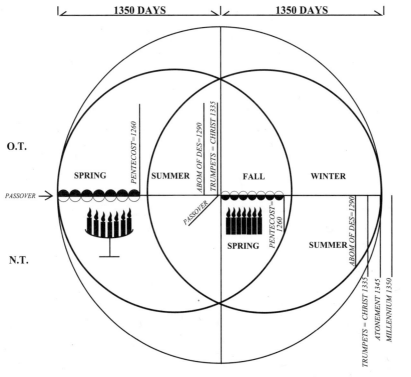

Figure 15

13
Gospel Versus Anti-Gospel

The gospel of the kingdom of God is the good news carried as light to a dark world. The light of that gospel radiates out as knowledge that illuminates heart and mind on how to have a proper relationship with God and man. Christ taught that the entire gospel rests on two great principles of the law. In Matthew 22:36-40 Christ summarized them when answering a question from a Pharisee. Matthew 22 verses 36-40: "'Teacher, which is the great commandment in the law?' Jesus said to him, 'You shall love the Lord your God with all your heart, with all your soul, and with all your mind. This is the first and great commandment. And the second is like it: You shall love your neighbor as yourself. On these two commandments hang all the Law and the Prophets.'"

Love toward God is the simplest way to summarize the first four of the Ten Commandments, and love toward our fellow man the simplest way to summarize the last six of the Ten Commandments. (See Exodus 20 and Deuteronomy 5 for the Ten Commandments.) In John 14:15 Christ said, "If you love Me, keep My commandments." Therefore, if we love God by keeping His commandments and the commandments teach us how to love Him and how to love our fellow men who are made in His image, love must be the ultimate source of light. I John 4:8 should not be surprising. "He who does not love does not know God, for God is love."

The Ten Commandments

The first four commandments teach us how to love God:

1. I am the Lord your God, who brought you out of the land of Egypt, out of the house of bondage. You shall have no other gods before Me.
2. You shall not make for yourself a carved image - any likeness of anything that is heaven above, or that is in the earth beneath, or that is in the water under the earth; you shall not bow down to them nor serve them.
3. You shall not take the name of the Lord your God in vain, for the Lord will not hold him guiltless who takes His name in vain.
4. Remember the Sabbath day, to keep it holy. Six days you shall labor and do all your work, but the seventh day is the Sabbath of the Lord your God.

The last six commandments teach us how to love our fellow man:

5. Honor your father and your mother, that your days may be long upon the land which the Lord your God is giving you.
6. You shall not murder.
7. You shall not commit adultery.
8. You shall not steal.
9. You shall not bear false witness against your neighbor.
10. You shall not covet your neighbor's house; you shall not covet your neighbor's wife, … nor anything that is your neighbor's.

(Exodus 20)

The two witnesses of the Old Testament and the New Testament must then all relate back to the love of God.

- It stands to reason, then, that the holy days are high Sabbaths demonstrating how God will lovingly deliver the human race from misery and tyranny. This is because the entire Bible is the living word of God, His breath on paper.
- The weekly Sabbath depicts how God will bless the world with one thousand years of peace with Satan's influence banished.
- Honoring God is obedience to His law, not to slander His name nor take it in vain.
- Honoring God requires that there be no idols in our lives whether that is a statue, a relic, money, or material possessions.
- It is wrong to portray God as a Being full of rage at the end of the age, willing to inflict pain and death on billions of people.

Logically, then, anything promoting something other than God's laws, His holy days, or His prophetic word is anti-love, anti-light, and anti-gospel, and therefore antichrist.

The ramifications of this understanding are enormous because any religion or personal dogma that is not substantiated in God's word is incorrect and in essence is part of an anti-gospel. God's word tells us in Revelation 12:9 that Satan has deceived the whole world, and how true that is.

It is easy for most of us to see the wrong in murder, theft, torture, and adultery, although many have committed these offenses. It is hard to recognize right from wrong and then choose to do right every time. Imagine for a moment how much harder it is to choose God's way when we cannot see why it should matter one way or the other. For example, why does it matter to:

- worship God on Saturday or Sunday?
- worship God on Passover or Easter?
- worship God on Atonement or celebrate Halloween?

- worship God at the Feast of Tabernacles or Christmas?
- worship God by praying before a statue or icon?
- worship God by worshipping creation?
- What is wrong with stealing from the rich and giving to the poor?
- What is wrong with jealousy and greed?
- What is wrong with violent entertainment since it is fake?
- Where does it stop; where do we draw the line? We need God to draw the lines, and He has done so in His word.

Not long after Christ passed the light to His Church, the forces of darkness were trying to put out the light. The Old Testament congregation was given a physical symbol of the light of the gospel, and that was the menorah. The seven candles each represented one week of prophetic years for a total of 1260 prophetic days. The seven candlesticks of Revelation 1:11 represent the seven weeks of prophetic years the Christian Church would struggle to carry the light of the gospel. This also totaled 1260 prophetic days. Revelation 1 verse 11: "…'I am the Alpha and the Omega, the First and the Last,' and, 'What you see, write in a book and send it to the seven churches which are in Asia: to Ephesus, to Smyrna, to Pergamos, to Thyatira, to Sardis, to Philadelphia, and to Laodicea.'"

In Revelation 1:9 John calls the struggle to keep the light of the gospel burning brightly, the tribulation: "I, John, both your brother and companion in the tribulation and kingdom and patience of Jesus Christ, was on the island that is called Patmos for the word of God and for the testimony of Jesus Christ." The struggle between the true gospel and the anti-gospel is the tribulation. Tribulation at its core is the struggle between light and dark, love and hate, truth and lies.

What Do You Mean Tribulation?

Tribulation: very few words conjure up more fear, anxiety and dread of what the future holds. This book will boldly dig into God's thoughts regarding tribulation. Set aside preconceived notions as we study God's thoughts on this subject. Let God explain from His word, the Bible, what the tribulation is and what He expects of us as we go through it.

The word "tribulation" is used 26 times in the Bible: four times in the Old Testament and 22 times in the New Testament. In the Old Testament "tribulation" comes from the Hebrew word *tsar* or *tsarah*. *Tsar* (#6862 Strong 1995) means a narrow, tight place, usually figuratively; also a pebble or stone as pressed hard by an opponent as if crowding. In the New Testament the word for "tribulation" is *thlipsis* which means "pressure (literally or figuratively)" (#2347 Strong 1995). It comes from the word *thlibo* "to crowd" (#2346 Strong 1995). These two words come from the word *tribos* (#5147 Strong 1995) which means to rub as if along a rut or worn track. We will refer back to these definitions as we study, but the first thing to notice is that they do not mean utter death and destruction. Many associate tribulation with the almost total annihilation of mankind in an end-time cataclysm. We will see the fallacy of that idea as we go along.

Since tribulation by definition is not synonymous with death and destruction, we must find out what it is. The first thing we will notice in God's word is that the tribulation had already started 2,000 years ago. The apostle John records in Revelation 1:9, "I, John, both your brother and companion in the **tribulation** and kingdom and patience of Jesus Christ, was on the island that is called Patmos for the word of God and for the testimony of Jesus Christ" (emphasis added). Therefore John and his brethren and companions were feeling the pressure of the **tribulation** 2,000 years ago! As a matter of fact, in verses 1-3 John records that the Book of Revelation was being given to him by Christ to help him and his brethren and companions to understand the things they were about to experience in their day: "The Revelation of Jesus Christ, which God gave Him to show His servants – things which must shortly take place. And He sent and signified it by His angel to His servant John, who bore witness to the word of God, and to the testimony of Jesus Christ, to all things that he saw. Blessed is he who reads and those who hear the words of this prophecy, and keep those things which are written in it; for the time is near." So the **tribulation** had started in John's day and continues till this very day! That is why ever since the Book of Revelation has been written, it has been a blessing to those who read, heard, and heeded its words. That is what God says in His word. We must believe and accept it. Let us gather some more scriptural evidence to back up John's claim that he was experiencing the **tribulation** in his time.

Christ directly warned His disciples of the **tribulation** in John 16 verse 33: "These things I have spoken to you, that in Me you may have peace. In the world you will have **tribulation**; but be of good cheer, I have overcome the world" (emphasis added). As he wrote Revelation, John knew he was in the tribulation because his Lord and Savior, Jesus Christ, told him he would experience it. The word Christ used for "world" here is *kosmos* (#2889 Strong 1995) which means the orderly arrangement, literally, figuratively or morally of the world. The base or root of this word is *komizo* (#2865 Strong 1995) which means the way the world is tended or cared for. Satan and his current world order are the source of tribulation.

Let's examine a few Scriptures that depict the fight between the gospel and the anti-gospel. We turn first to the apostle Paul's words about how the effort to preach the gospel would be accomplished. Romans 10 verses 14-18: "How then shall they call on Him in whom they have not believed? And how should they believe in Him of whom they have not heard? And how shall they hear without a preacher? And how shall they preach unless they are sent? As it is written: 'How beautiful are the feet of those who preach the gospel of peace, who bring glad tidings of good things!' But they have not all obeyed the gospel. For Isaiah says, 'Lord, who has believed our report?' So then faith comes by hearing, and hearing by the word of God. But I say, have they not heard? Yes indeed: 'Their sound has gone out to all the earth, and their words to the ends of the world.'" Note that verse 15 quotes Isaiah 52:7 and verse 18 quotes Psalm 19:4, both references from the first witness, the Old Testament.

In II Corinthians 11:1-4, Paul actually refers to a false gospel that he worries may deceive the brethren: "Oh, that you would bear with me in a little folly - and indeed you do bear with me. For I am jealous for you with godly jealously. For I have betrothed you to one husband, that I may present you as a chaste virgin to Christ. But I fear, lest somehow, as the serpent deceived Eve by his craftiness, so your minds may be corrupted from the simplicity that is in Christ. For if he who comes preaches another Jesus whom we have not preached, or if you receive a different spirit which you have not received, or a different gospel which you have not accepted - you may well put up with it!" This verse confirms that it is Satan who is behind trying to deceive God's woman once again, just as he deceived Eve into accepting his lies.

In II Thessalonians 2:7 Paul refers to these deceptions as "the mystery of lawlessness" or as the King James Version says, the "mystery of iniquity": "For the mystery of lawlessness is already at work; only He who now restrains will do so until He is taken out of the way."

This mysterious power was already at work in Paul's day - that is what the Scripture says. By reading the entire context in II Thessalonians 2:1-11, it is clear that Paul was addressing the fears of some people at the time that Christ had already secretly returned. Paul carefully explains not to fear because first there must be a notable apostasy from the truth within God's true Church, promulgated by the abomination of desolation. He expresses the abomination of desolation in the holy place (Matthew 24:15) in somewhat different terms. He refers to the abomination of desolation as the son of perdition (none other than Satan) sitting in the temple. Now we read II Thessalonians 2 verses 1-11: "Now, brethren, concerning the coming of our Lord Jesus Christ and our gathering together to Him, we ask you, not to be soon shaken in mind or troubled, either by spirit or by word or by letter, as if from us, as though the day of Christ had come. Let no one deceive you by any means; for that Day will not come unless the falling away comes first, and the man of sin is revealed, the son of perdition, who opposes and exalts himself above all that is called God or that is worshipped, so that he sits as God in the temple of God, showing himself that he is God. Do you not remember that when I was still with you I told you these things? And now you know what is restraining, that he may be revealed in his own time. For the mystery of lawlessness is already at work; only He who now restrains will do so until He is taken out of the way. And then the lawless one will be revealed, whom the Lord will consume with the breath of His mouth and destroy with the brightness of His coming. The coming of the lawless one is according to the working of Satan, with all power, signs, and lying wonders, and with all unrighteous deception among those who perish, because they did not receive the love of the truth, that they might be saved. And for this reason God will send them strong delusion that they should believe the lie."

Satan obviously uses false signs and lying wonders to deceive the Church into accepting a false gospel *after* the true gospel has gone forth to the world as a witness.

Satan cunningly replaces God's signs and wonders with the physical signs of wars, rumors of wars, famines, earthquakes, etc. (Matthew 24:4-7), directing attention away from God and onto personal survival:

- He changes God's laws on how to relate to Him, corrupting the first three commandments.
- He substitutes God's prophetic calendar, holy days, and Sabbath with pagan celebrations, so people have no way of tracking prophetic time and fulfillments.
- He usurps the use of God's word, twisting it into a gospel of death and destruction instead of the good news of peace and liberty. He has the audacity to think he can impose his own will for the human race over God's.
- Comprehension of Satan's diabolical plan is what begins to reveal the son of perdition for all the world to see. Isaiah 14 verses 12-17: "How you are fallen from heaven, O Lucifer, son of the morning! How you are cut down to the ground, you who weakened the nations! For you

have said in your heart: 'I will ascend into heaven, I will exalt my throne above the stars of God; I will also sit on the mount of the congregation on the farthest sides of the north; I will ascend above the heights of the clouds, I will be like the Most High.' Yet you shall be brought down to Sheol, to the lowest depths of the Pit. Those who see you will gaze at you, and consider you, saying: 'Is this the man who made the earth tremble, who shook kingdoms, who made the world as a wilderness and destroyed its cities, who did not open the house of his prisoners?'"

- The holy day that pictures the utter defeat of Satan's realm is the Day of Atonement.
- Finally, Satan succeeded in his effort to get God's people to turn on each other, devouring the body of Christ. A body that should be known by its love for one another (John 13:34-35) has seen the love of many wax cold (Matthew 24:12). The last days have seen the Church break down into competing factions that often accuse, slander, and divide rather than heal and forgive. This sad state of affairs is what has ultimately led to a loss of spiritual vision and the ability to preach the truth, thus fulfilling an enigmatic prophecy in Zechariah 14 verses 12-13: "And this shall be the plague with which the Lord will strike all the people who fought against Jerusalem: their flesh shall dissolve while they stand on their feet, their eyes shall dissolve in their sockets, and their tongues shall dissolve in their mouths. It shall come to pass in that day that a great panic from the Lord will be among them. Everyone will seize the hand of his neighbor, and raise his hand against his neighbor's hand."

A Brief History of the Mystery of Iniquity

For far too long people have tried to identify the son of perdition by attaching the title to a human being. Logic says that is impossible. Satan is the only personification that makes sense.

We have already seen in Scripture that the mystery of iniquity was already at work in Paul's time two thousand years ago. This evil spirit does not succeed in shutting down the two witnesses until the end of the age. No human being can live two thousand years. Satan and his demons, chiefly the four horsemen of the Apocalypse, have been behind the war on truth ever since deceiving the first woman, Eve, in the garden of Eden.

In various places the Bible shows where Satan's attack on the gospel is coming from by identifying the person, city, nation, or kingdom he is using at the time. The following examples will help illustrate this.

- In Isaiah 14:3-12 Satan is identified as Lucifer, king of Babylon.
- Ezekiel 28:11-17 calls Satan the king of Tyre.
- John 17:12 calls Judas, Christ's betrayer, the son of perdition *once Satan had entered him* (John 13:27, Luke 22:3).
- In Matthew 16:23, Jesus even called the apostle Peter Satan, identifying the source of the anti-gospel idea he was espousing. Let's read Matthew 16 verses 21-23: "From that time Jesus began to show His disciples that He must go to Jerusalem, and suffer many things from the elders and chief priests and scribes, and be killed, and be raised the third day. Then Peter took Him aside and began to rebuke Him, saying, 'Far be it from You, Lord; this shall not happen to You!' But He turned and said to Peter, 'Get behind Me, Satan! You are an offense to Me, for you are not mindful of the things of God, but the things of men.'"

It is clear that the person, city, or nation is not the mystery of iniquity. Satan is the son of perdition using them, usually without their knowledge. When it is with their knowledge and consent, as in the case of Judas, as opposed to Peter, then that person is indeed in danger of being a "son" of wickedness. This is explained by Christ when He discusses the wheat and tares in Matthew 13:36-

43. Very, very few people fall into this category. It is important to stress this point because the overwhelming majority of people on earth want to do what is right. We did not choose our parents, our ethnicity, culture, or nation of birth. It really serves no good purpose to point to another human as the son of perdition, another nation as the great Satan, or another culture or religion as evil. Reserve those descriptions for Satan, his four chief horsemen, and his demons.

Having said all that, we can look at history rationally and see where and when Satan chose to attack the true gospel and substitute a false one. Christ had been dead less than twenty years when Paul wrote in II Thessalonians 2 that the mystery of iniquity was already at work.

The apostle Luke records a bizarre episode of a famous magician trying to "buy the Holy Spirit" after successfully getting baptized into the Church. One Simon Magus was considered a god by many people of his day, notably the Samaritans. This Simon saw that the spiritual power at work in the apostles was greater than his own, and he lusted after it. Let's read this account in Acts 8 verses 9-25: "But there was a certain man called Simon, who previously practiced sorcery in the city and astonished the people of Samaria, claiming that he was someone great, to whom they all gave heed, from the least to the greatest, saying, 'This man is the great power of God.' And they heeded him because he had astonished them with his sorceries for a long time. But when they believed Phillip as he preached the things concerning the kingdom of God and the name of Jesus Christ, both men and women were baptized. Then Simon himself also believed; and when he was baptized he continued with Phillip, and was amazed, seeing the miracles and signs which were done. Now when the apostles who were at Jerusalem heard that Samaria had received the word of God, they sent Peter and John to them, who, when they had come down, prayed for them that they might receive the Holy Spirit. For as yet He had fallen upon none of them. They had only been baptized in the name of the Lord Jesus. Then they laid hands on them, and they received the Holy Spirit. And when Simon saw that through the laying on of the apostles' hands the Holy Spirit was given, he offered them money, saying, 'Give me this power also, that anyone on whom I lay hands may receive the Holy Spirit.' But Peter said to him, 'Your money perish with you, because you thought that the gift of God could be purchased with money.'"

Peter perceived what Simon Magus was up to, and refused to lay hands on him to call the Holy Spirit onto him. The Spirit cannot be purchased, and power or position cannot be obtained politically in God's Church. Peter concluded his strong rebuke of Simon Magus in verse 23 with the words, "'For I see that you are poisoned by bitterness and bound by *iniquity*'" (emphasis added). Clearly the mystery of iniquity was at work in this man, and he was cooperating with that spirit to the point of allowing people to believe he possessed the power of God and that he was a god. This was the first evidence of Satan trying to enter the spiritual temple of God's Church after Christ's death and resurrection. It has always been Satan's goal to be on a par with God, even to be considered a third god along with God the Father and Jesus Christ.

Satan had the brazenness to think he might even get Christ to allow him into the Godhead by working a deal with Him in what is known as "the temptation in the wilderness." Matthew 4:1-11 relays the amazing story of how Satan tried to exchange the world he held captive for a position. It would have been his by default if Christ had obeyed Satan, worshiped him, or traded earth "as is" without His shed blood. That is how diabolical the son of perdition truly is.

The expression that Peter used in Acts 8:23, "poisoned by bitterness," is better translated "in the gall of bitterness" in the King James Version. This is an Old Testament concept for switching true worship for idolatry. This was a cardinal sin breaking the first three commandments that Moses and the people covenanted with God to keep. Read about it in Deuteronomy 29:1, 12-18. "These are the words of the covenant which the Lord commanded Moses to make with the children of Israel in the land of Moab, besides the covenant which He made with them in Horeb. ...that you may enter into covenant with the Lord your God, and into His oath, which the Lord your God makes with you today, that He may establish you today as a people for Himself, and that He may be God to you, just as He has spoken to you, and just as He has sworn to your fathers, to Abraham, Isaac, and Jacob. I make this covenant and this oath, not with you alone, but with Him who stands here with us today before the Lord our God, as well as with him who is not here with us today (for you know that we dwelt in the land of Egypt and that we came through the nations which you passed by, and you saw their abominations and their idols which were among them - wood and stone and silver and gold); so that there may not be among you man or woman or family or tribe, whose heart turns away today from the Lord our God, to go and serve the gods of these nations, and that there may not be among you a root bearing bitterness or wormwood."

"Wormwood" comes from the Hebrew *laanah* (#3939 Strong 1995) meaning to curse, wormwood as poisonous, and accursed. The New Testament uses the word "wormwood" in Revelation 8:11 to depict a name for Satan's star and how it pollutes the clear waters of the gospel: "The name of the star is Wormwood. A third of the waters became wormwood, and many men died from the water, because it was made bitter."

The word "gall" as used in Acts 8:23 comes from the Greek word *chole* (#5521 Strong 1995), meaning poison in type, wormwood. Therefore, substitution of any part of the gospel of the kingdom or the laws it is founded on, or the prophetic time kept by the true signs and wonders, constitutes wormwood or gall. The son of perdition operating as the mystery of iniquity is the source of poisonous venom. The antidote is the true gospel of the kingdom contained within the two witnesses.

The next big assault on the truth was at the Council of Nicea in 325 A.D. At this famous council, called by Emperor Constantine of Rome, the debates raged between adherents to the true gospel of the kingdom and those adhering to the anti-gospel.

Constantine's main agenda was to preserve what was left of the Roman Empire by unifying its far-flung peoples, faiths, and cultures under one religion. While clerics from both sides argued their cases before him, Constantine (under influence of the god of this world) threw the weight of his authority behind the wrong gospel. A powerful union of church and state pushed the bulk of Christianity in the wrong direction while severely persecuting the small group of Christians who looked "Jewish" to them. The Romans and Jewish zealots had fought many, many times. The abomination and desolation in Jerusalem in 70 A.D. by Titus of Rome was the most notable. Neither Constantine nor the believers in the anti-gospel understood that one cannot physically kill a spiritual entity. Crucifixion did not stop Christ. Persecution, tribulation, and death could not stop the body of Christ, or the bride of Christ, or the Church of Christ. Even though Constantine proclaimed God's Sabbath and holy days illegal and punishable by death, he could not stop God's loving thoughts embodied in the gospel of the kingdom from being passed from generation to generation for 1260 prophetic days.

Though many true Christians suffered and died because of Constantine's decree, it was the legitimacy given the false gospel that would hound the Church for nearly 1700 years. Doctrines adopted at the Council of Nicea have opposed the true gospel at every turn. According to *World Book Encyclopedia*, 1983 Edition, doctrines adopted at the Council of Nicea included:

- Substituting Easter Sunday for Passover determined by God's calendar (See articles on Nicea, Council of, and Easter.)
- The doctrine of the Trinity which opened the God-head to admit one more (See articles on Nicea, Council of, and Trinity.)
- -Icons and images of Jesus Christ and saints were allowed, breaking the first and second commandments. This doctrine was permanently established at the second Council of Nicea in 787 A.D. (See article on iconology.)

The Councils of Nicea in 325 and 787 are two of 21 ecumenical councils that helped set doctrine and decide issues for the government-sanctioned Christianity. Satan's fight against the true gospel did make it very difficult to spread the good news to the whole world, which made tribulation a reality for God's people. But when dealing with Satan, even unknowingly, there are unintended negative consequences.

Government-sanctioned Christianity eventually led to the crusades, the inquisition, the holocaust, and interminable fighting between Catholics and Protestants, Christians and Muslims, Christians and Jews. Most of the wars were fought invoking the name of God. Sometimes they even pitted men of the same faith in bloody battles against each other while both sides were "blessed" by the church. We have paid a horrible price for losing sight of the true gospel of the kingdom.

Humanity has finally realized the point in time when all of our divisions will be healed and the true source of our miseries exposed, which is Satan and his demonic realm.

The Seven Church Eras

The Book of Revelation is the story of how the gospel of the kingdom reached the whole world as a witness and then will go on to convert the whole world. Revelation is the fascinating history, written in advance, of the successes and failures, trials and tribulation, and the ultimate triumph of the people charged with carrying the light of the gospel to the whole world. It is the chronicle of God's light prevailing over the forces of darkness and ignorance - a goal first stated in Genesis 1: "Let there be light." Genesis and Revelation are the book ends holding the history of the spiritual war between good and evil. The war is almost over.

The work of bringing the light of the gospel to the world was passed from the Old Testament congregation of Israel to the New Testament Church. The torch was taken from the prophets and Levitical priesthood by Christ and handed off to the twelve disciples gathered on the first Pentecost A.D. Isaiah 42:6-7 calls the people of Israel to be a light to the world: "I, the Lord, have called You in righteousness, and will hold Your hand; I will keep You and give You as a covenant to the people, as a light to the Gentiles, to open blind eyes, to bring out prisoners from the prison, those who sit in darkness from the prison house." The most enduring symbol of Israel's mission to be a light to the world is the menorah, the golden lampstand in the form of a tree with seven branches holding seven lamps fueled by pure olive oil. Instructions for building the golden lampstands were given to Moses by God (Exodus 25:31-40, 37:17-24) at Mount Sinai on the first Pentecost in the Old Testament. That remarkable symbol of the Old Testament gospel, the first witness, glowing within God's people, was eventually placed in the sanctuary of Solomon's temple. There it burned every day until the abomination of desolation at the hands of Nebuchadnezzar, king of Babylon. The menorah had burned for nearly one thousand years, the last four hundred of which were in the temple. Prophetically this was the first fulfillment of 1260 days or seven weeks of prophetic years (7 X 360 divided by 2), the conclusion of spiritual springtime for ancient Israel.

It should not be surprising that the two witnesses of the New Testament Church work for 1260 prophetic times and are symbolized by seven candlesticks/lamps. In Matthew 5 Christ called His disciples "the light of the world," a lamp that should shine for the whole world (Matthew 5:14-16). Revelation 1:12-13 pictures the New Testament Church as seven lampstands. The mission of the Church to take the gospel of the kingdom to the world as a witness meant they would have to keep the truth burning for 1260 prophetic days (7 X 360 divided by 2). That is why Christ chose seven congregations of the early Church to receive copies of the Book of Revelation. Within the book each would receive a letter addressed to them. Each letter contained information applicable to them and to the subsequent eras of the Church. Each era was to bear one of their names. The letters were physically delivered to the seven Churches who were located along an old Roman mail route in the part of Asia now known as Turkey. The prophetic parts of the letters were to be "opened" to the understanding of their future namesake eras. Christ would send the revealed information by His angels at the appropriate time. Each Church era was to be served by a specific angel. Now let's see the supporting Scriptures for this from Revelation 1.

- Revelation 1:1-3 - revelation of Christ sent by an angel
- Revelation 1:4 - given to John for seven Churches
- Revelation 1:9-11 – John, who was already suffering in the tribulation, hears the message through the voice of an angel sounding like a trumpet.
- Revelation 1:18-20 - Christ was sending information to John about some things that had already happened, were happening, and would happen.

Understanding that Revelation has been in the process of being fulfilled ever since Christ's resurrection is very comforting. Too many ministers and scholars have tried to compress nearly the entire book into some horrible end-time tribulation that some say lasts three and one-half years and others seven years in duration. In actual fact, by far most of the prophecies of Revelation are now history. They have passed! They did not understand the prophetic times and seasons, so they misapplied 1260 prophetic days.

Too many people have viewed the letters to the seven Churches in chapters 2 and 3 as each Church's entire letter. Actually chapters 2 and 3 contain a salutation and preface to each Church era with more information in the rest of the book. Valuable prophetic knowledge for each era is carefully arranged chronologically and by subject to be helpful at the right time. Some information is for a specific era or eras, and some applies to them all. Reading the book of Revelation with this in mind is a huge step in the direction of clarity. It is also a soothing balm to the jangled nerves of an anxious world. It is amazing how many people are fearful of events long past. It is sad how many people are needlessly terrified by the Book of Revelation's symbolism. Revelation was inspired by the Holy Spirit, and II Timothy 1:7 tells us, "For God has not given us a spirit of fear, but of power and of love and of a sound mind." A good understanding of Revelation will allay our fears and give us sounder minds.

The Book of Revelation is prophetic history of how God will redeem the earth. The earth is saved in three stages. See Chapter 4 and Figure 2 in Chapter 8. The first stage is from the Garden of Eden until Moses. In this period of time, roughly two thousand years, the fruit of the earth is limited to the patriarchs. They are mentioned in Revelation 4 and 5 as the elders redeemed of the earth but not resurrected to eternal life until Christ's second coming.

The second stage is from Moses at Mount Sinai until Christ. During this period, the earth's bounty is limited to the prophets. They were set aside as saints at their death and await the resurrection. They briefly came back to life at Christ's resurrection (Matthew 27:51-53). They are spoken of in Revelation 6:9-11 as revealed when Christ opens the fifth seal. Therefore, the events of the fifth seal took place two thousand years ago.

From that point the Book of Revelation repeatedly takes us through the work of the Church to take the gospel to the world as a witness. Each time it does this, it concludes with the redemption of the whole earth. This is observed in Revelation 7 in which 144,000 are redeemed first, then the innumerable multitude. The same thing is in Revelation 11 and 14 and Revelation 19:1-10, where the firstfruits are redeemed, then the world at large. In each case the prophetic 1260 days in which the Church works as Christ's helpmate is covered in more detail. Therefore, since we learned earlier what is meant by the 1260 and 1290 days, it is obvious that most of the Book of Revelation has been fulfilled. Remember the Book of Revelation is predominately composed of messages to the Church, opened to understanding at the right time. The message of the gospel of the kingdom is now set to go to the entire world. Knowledge of God's plan of salvation, embodied in His holy days and prophetic calendar, will become common knowledge. Isaiah 60:1-5 speaks of this time beginning now as the time of the earth's conversion, when the masses of the sea of mankind are given ears to hear and eyes to see. It has been a long slog from Mount Sinai until the gospel of the kingdom reached the entire world as a witness. Prophetic time is now about to pick up great speed, as everything is now in place to make that possible. Man's knowledge has grown immensely, Bibles are everywhere, and communication is instantaneous.   Determining that the seven Churches of Revelation span approximately two thousand years is relatively easy. The apostle John received the prophecy of Revelation while living in exile on the Island of Patmos. According to the *Jamieson, Fausset, and Brown Commentary*, 1871, it is not absolutely clear which Roman emperor had exiled him, Nero or Domitian. Drawing on the *Ecclesiastical History* by the historian Eusebius, they state that upon Domitian's death, John was released from Patmos and went to live in Ephesus. Ephesus was the first city on the mail route of the seven Churches and the first Church era.

John, of all people, would have understood the importance of keeping the gospel of the kingdom pure. He was the last surviving apostle of Christ. He would have most certainly understood the significance of this prophecy from which he would teach to the Ephesians. In Revelation 1:1-3 he knew that message's first warning was that the time was near and would shortly begin to take place. In verse 9 he refers to himself as a brother in the tribulation. Lastly, in verse 19 he well knew that he had been inspired to "write the things which you have seen, and the things which are, and the things which will take place after this." Therefore he went to Ephesus as the last eyewitness to the life and times of Christ. From then on, the work of the Church took place in the wilderness away from physical Jerusalem. He was a witness of Christ's ministry with all its signs and wonders, His Passover sacrifice, and the marvels of Pentecost. He was well aware of a growing false gospel about Christ and His apostles. The letter to Ephesus, penned by his own hand, contained both praise and warning. Let's read this letter in its entirety (Revelation 2:1-7): "To the angel of the church of Ephesus write, 'These things says He who holds the seven stars in His right hand, who walks in the midst of the seven golden lampstands: I know your works, your labor, your patience, and that you cannot bear with those who are evil. And you have tested those who say they are apostles and are not, and have found them liars; and you have persevered and have patience, and have labored for My name's sake and have not become weary. Nevertheless I have this against you, that you have left your first love. Remember therefore from where you have fallen; repent and do the first works, or else I will come to you quickly and remove your lamp stand from its place – unless you repent. But this you have, that you hate the deeds of the Nicolaitans, which I also hate. He who has an ear, let him hear what the Spirit says to the churches. To him who overcomes I will give to eat from the tree of life, which is in the midst of the Paradise of God.'" By his own hand he wrote that this Church area and era had worked hard to preserve the truth, defend Christ's name, and fight heresy, but they were beginning to lose their zeal – their first love. If not corrected, those problems would cause the job of keepers of the flame of truth to soon pass to another area and era – Smyrna.

John's disciple Polycarp was next to assume the mantle of leadership. He kept the light of the gospel burning at the city of Smyrna until he was martyred there in 168 A.D.

Whereas the first era, Ephesus, was struggling against those who called themselves apostles but were liars (think Simon Magus, for example), Thyatira had a more systemic problem. Some believers had begun following the false apostles and their adulterated gospel. Paul was very concerned that might happen and expressed his fears in II Corinthians 11 verses 1-4: "Oh, that you would bear with me in a little folly - and indeed you do bear with me. For I am jealous for you with godly jealously. For I have betrothed you to one husband, that I may present you as a chaste virgin to Christ. But I fear, lest somehow, as the serpent deceived Eve by his craftiness, so your minds may be corrupted from the simplicity that is in Christ. For if he who comes preaches another Jesus whom we have not preached, or if you receive a different spirit which you have not received, or a different gospel which you have not accepted - you may well put up with it!"

Jesus Christ Himself warned of tares that would sprout and grow amidst His seed which He called the sons of God. He called the tares sons of the devil. (Review the parable of the wheat and tares Matthew 13:24-30 and Christ's explanation of it in Matthew 13:36-43). The Greek word for tares is *zizanion* meaning "false grain" (#2215 Strong 1995).

Smyrna is found to be dealing with false grain taking root within the Church which Christ refers to as "the synagogue of Satan." We will read about it in Revelation 2 verses 8-11: "And to the angel of the church in Smyrna write, 'These things says the First and the Last, who was dead and came to life: I know your works, tribulation, and poverty (but you are rich); and I know the blasphemy of those who say they are Jews and are not, but are a synagogue of Satan. Do not fear any of those things which you are about to suffer. Indeed, the devil is about to throw some of you into prison, that you may be tested, and you will have tribulation ten days. Be faithful until death, and I will give you the crown of life. He who has an ear, let him hear what the Spirit says to the churches. He who overcomes shall not be hurt by the second death.'"

Notice that Christ says that He is aware of their blasphemy, so it is what they *say* that is dangerous. They preach a different gospel. Paul explicitly warned of this in II Corinthians 11:1-4.

The reference to these false teachers as "the synagogue of Satan" does not mean these people are Jewish in physical ancestry. It is true that the Ephesian era was mostly composed of Jews. Christ was Jewish, the apostles were all Jewish, and the first three thousand converts on the initial Pentecost were all Jewish. Paul was given the commission to take the gospel to the Gentiles which he did with diligence and dispatch. The gospel very quickly spread to the non-Jewish world. Paul explains in Romans 2:28-29 that the Church, in essence, is composed of Jews "in spirit." Christianity is the spiritual out growth of the physical Jewish faith. That is precisely why there are former physical fulfillments and latter spiritual fulfillments of the holy days. It is important to grasp this because a misunderstanding of "synagogue of Satan" and other similar Scriptures has led many sincere people down the path of anti-Semitism.

The main point of this chapter is that the Church composed of seven Church eras was constantly struggling to keep out the false gospel for 1260 prophetic days.

The Council of Nicea brought the conflict between the two gospels out into the open. Once the backing of Roman civil authority was behind the wrong gospel, the vast majority of Christians took a wrong fork in the road. What developed was an incomplete and adulterated form of Christianity quite unlike what Christ founded on that first Pentecost. In order to not appear Jewish, times and laws were changed fulfilling the prophecy of Daniel 7 verse 25: "He shall speak pompous words against the Most High, shall persecute the saints of the Most High, and shall intend to change times and law. Then the saints shall be given into his hand for a time and times and half a time." In other words, they fight with Satan over the gospel for 1260 prophetic days.

Spiritual Calendar

A different spiritual calendar was instituted, different holy days observed, and God's Ten Commandment law changed to suit the adopted old pagan doctrines.

What has come to be known as "mainstream Christianity" has worked over the centuries to correct errors from the past. Many denominations splintered off as they identified certain wrong doctrines. Almost all Christian denominations have encouraged compassion, forgiveness, and philanthropy. At the same time, they have stubbornly clung to their rights to wage war, worship God on days He has not ordained, and determine dogma and doctrine not based on Scripture. Completely pure love of God and neighbor would preclude such behaviors. However, the world has benefited to the extent they have adhered in principle to the last six commandments. With their moral compass set on these, an ethic of hard work, human rights, strong families, and freedom of religion has been a great blessing. Perhaps their greatest achievement has been to put millions of Bibles into the hands of the common man in their own tongues. This will make it possible for an innumerable multitude of every nation, kindred, tongue, and people to come to know the true gospel of Christ (Revelation 7:9-10). The earth now verges on that point.

Returning to the seven eras, we want to learn more about the struggle between the gospel and anti-gospel. The next two Church eras are found to be battling long-dead foes. This is a strong indicator of history repeating itself. Pergamos is the next era, and they are warned that some among them hold the doctrines of Balaam who taught Balak how to trick Israel. These two men had actually lived almost two thousand years before Pergamos. They were first mentioned in the Bible in the Old Testament book of Numbers chapters 22-24 before Israel had even finished wandering in the desert. Like Simon Magus, Balaam was a magician or sorcerer for hire. You can look up the lengthy Old Testament account yourself, but we will read this message to Pergamos in Revelation 2 verses 12-16: "And to the angel of the church in Pergamos write, 'These things says He who has the sharp two-edged sword: I know your works, and where you dwell, where Satan's throne is. And you hold fast to My name, and did not deny My faith even in the days in which Antipas was My faithful martyr, who was killed among you, where Satan dwells. But I have a few things against you, because you have there those who hold the doctrine of Balaam, who taught Balak to put a stumbling block before the children of Israel, to eat things sacrificed to idols, and to commit sexual immorality. Thus you also have those who hold the doctrine of the Nicolaitans, which thing I hate. Repent, or else I will come to you quickly and will fight against them with the sword of My mouth.'"

Balaam and Balak were long dead, but the evil spirits working in their lives never die. They live on to wage war with God's people. Balaam's name means devourer of the people, and Balak means one who destroys. This is exactly what they colluded to do through false divination and cursing. They tried to harm God's people by false prophecy and testimony. It was one of Satan's earliest attempts to stop Israel from carrying the light of the gospel.

Thyatira was the next Church era, and she also struggled against a spirit that long ago plagued God's people. The Old Testament book of I Kings chapters 18-21 details how God's prophet Elijah defeated the false prophets of Baal. Baal was the name of an ancient Phoenician god whose name means possessor or controller, master or husband: in other words, Satan the god of this world. Evil queen Jezebel was a big supporter of the prophets of Baal who tried to kill God's prophet Elijah for what he had done. Jezebel means "chaste" (#348 Strong 1995), but she was far from it. Just considering the meaning of their names gives us a clue that Thyatira was fighting a form of immoral spiritual deceit.

Now we read the message to Thyatira in Revelation 2 verses 18-25: "And to the angel of the church in Thyatira write, 'These things says the Son of God, who has eyes like a flame of fire, and His feet like fine brass: I know your works, love, service, faith, and your patience; and as for your works, the last are more than the first. Nevertheless I have a few things against you, because you allow that woman Jezebel, who calls herself a prophetess, to teach and seduce My servants to commit sexual immorality and eat things sacrificed to idols. And I gave her time to repent of her sexual immorality, and she did not repent. Indeed I will cast her into a sick-bed, and those who commit adultery with her into great tribulation, unless they repent of their deeds. I will kill her children with death, and all the churches shall know that I am He who searches the minds and hearts. And I will give to each one of you according to your works. Now to you I say, and to the rest in Thyatira, as many as do not have this doctrine, who have not known the depths of Satan, as they say, I will put on you no other burden. But hold fast what you have till I come.'"

When God's woman, the Church, dabbles in Satan's pagan doctrines, Christ considers it a spiritual form of sexual immorality. It is important to note that the chronological order of Balak, Balaam, and Jezebel in Revelation 2 is the same as the Old Testament occurrences.

The next Church to receive a message is Sardis, sometimes known as the "dead Church" because they had lost so much of the truth of the gospel. This is the small Church that Herbert W. Armstrong became part of in the 1920's. These sincere people kept the seventh day Sabbath, did not make or worship statues or icons, and did not celebrate pagan holy days. But they had lost knowledge of God's holy days. For the most part, God had turned away from them.

The Philadelphia era was to be the one to accomplish taking the gospel of the kingdom to the whole world as a witness, fulfilling Christ's prophecy in Matthew 24:14. Now let's read the message to Philadelphia (Revelation 3:7-13): "And to the angel of the church in

Philadelphia write, 'These things says He who is holy, who is true, He who has the key of David, He who opens and no one shuts, and shuts and no one opens: I know your works. See, I have set before you an open door, and no one can shut it; for you have a little strength, have kept My word, and have not denied My name. Indeed I will make those of the synagogue of Satan, who says they are Jews and are not, but lie - indeed I will make them come and worship before your feet, and to know that I have loved you. Because you have kept My command to persevere, I will also keep you from the hour of trial which shall come upon the whole world, to test those who dwell on the earth. Behold, I am coming quickly! Hold fast what you have, that no one may take your crown. He who overcomes, I will make him a pillar in the temple of My God, and He shall go out no more. I will write on him the name of My God and the name of the city of My God, the New Jerusalem, which comes down out of heaven from My God. And I will write on him My new name. He who has an ear, let him hear what the Spirit says to the churches.'"

This small Church did indeed take the gospel of the kingdom to the entire world as a witness. In Chapter 12 we briefly covered the life and times of Herbert Armstrong. It is undeniable that he accomplished this mission. What is not so well known is how he and his wife restored the knowledge of God's holy days to the Church. These are the very holy days forced underground at the Council of Nicea in 325. They are the same holy days that Christ, the disciples, and the early Church observed. God's holy days are a critical part of the gospel of the kingdom. Fulfillment of these days, as we have demonstrated from Scripture, is God's step-by-step plan to deliver mankind from Satan's tyranny. Fulfillment of the holy days preserves this earth for a wonderful Millennium just ahead.

Christ spoke of the restoration of the full gospel as the work of a person to come in the same spirit and power of Elijah that defeated the prophets of Baal and Jezebel in the Old Testament. Mark 9:11-13 refers to an Elijah yet to come even though the prophet Elijah served God more than 500 years earlier. Let's read the exchange between Christ and His disciples: "And they asked Him, saying,

'Why do the scribes say that Elijah must come first?' Then He answered and told them, 'Indeed, Elijah is coming first and restores all things. And how is it written concerning the Son of Man, that He must suffer many things and be treated with contempt? But I say to you that Elijah has also come, and they did to him whatever they wished, as it is written of him.'"

The Book of Malachi is a prophecy written in the fifth century B.C., more than two hundred years after Elijah. Yet in Malachi 4:5-6, Malachi speaks of an Elijah to cause remembrance of the law and statutes, which includes the holy days. By doing so, he would turn the hearts of God the Father (should be singular in translation) to His children and the hearts of the children to Him. This averts a curse that would otherwise befall the earth. Curse in Hebrew is *cherem* (#2764 Strong 1995), meaning utter doom and extermination. Yes, without God's fulfilled plan, the earth was doomed. Mankind would obliterate the planet by the inventions of his mind under Satan's influence. God intends that this will never happen. Setting mankind free from Satan's influence is critical. Therefore, knowledge of the true gospel of the kingdom will soon steer humanity away from Satan and toward Christ. The light of the gospel has now been carried through the entire first fulfillment and nearly the entire second fulfillment. So many pieces of this prophetic puzzle are now in place that all that is required is a little spiritual vision and hearing. Thanks to the enormous sacrifices of those who have gone before, we are now experiencing a veritable explosion of biblical knowledge.

Remember how Daniel was told by the angel (Daniel 12:4,7) that his prophecy would be sealed until the time of the end when people would run to and fro and knowledge would increase. The increase in knowledge is both in physical and spiritual terms, and that time is now!

We now come to the Laodicean era, the one in which we live now. This is the era to follow the preaching of the gospel of the kingdom to the world as a witness. Therefore this is the era to live through the abomination of desolation and the collapse of the two witnesses. Revelation 3:14-19 describes their condition and what Christ tells them to do about it: "And to the angel of the church of the Laodiceans write, 'These things says the Amen, the Faithful and True Witness, the Beginning of the creation of God: I know your works, that you are neither cold nor hot. I wish you were cold or hot. So then, because you are lukewarm, and neither cold nor hot, I will vomit you out of My mouth. Because you say, "I am rich, have become wealthy, and have need of nothing" – and do not know that you are wretched, miserable, poor, blind, and naked – I counsel you to buy from Me gold refined in the fire, that you may be rich; and white garments, that you may be clothed, that the shame of your nakedness may not be revealed; and anoint your eyes with eye salve, that you may see. As many as I love, I rebuke and chasten. Therefore be zealous and repent.'"

The statement by Christ in verse 20 shows how close this is to His return. "Behold, I stand at the door and knock. If anyone hears my voice and opens the door, I will come in to him and dine with him, and he with Me." This is the era that Satan overcomes, starting on the 1290th day. The 1290th day pictures when the false gospel, sanctioned by the Roman Empire in 325, becomes official doctrine in the Church. The Church is not a physical entity but rather a spiritual body, the temple of God. The spiritual work of the two witnesses and the light of the gospel must, however, work through physical entities, i.e. organized churches, corporations, and congregations. Just as Christ told the Pharisees so long ago, "not what goes into the mouth defiles a man; but what comes out of the mouth" (Matthew 15:11), so it is at the end of the age. The son of perdition sitting in the temple of God showing himself that he is God (II Thessalonians 2) is evidenced by what comes out of the Church.

At the end of the age, the Church dissolved into three major divisions with many subdivisions:

- Those who stopped believing all together.

- Those who began to preach once again the false gospel from the Council of Nicea.

- Those who still kept the Sabbath and the holy days, but preached the gospel of death and destruction and a horrible end-time fate for mankind.

For a short time, it has appeared as if the four horsemen of the Apocalypse may well have won. This is characterized in Revelation 11 as the two witnesses being dead for three and one-half days. This is a period in which they are not buried, for one cannot kill the truth and bury it, only change the gospel into the anti-gospel. However, Satan cannot beat God. When he succeeded in having Roman soldiers kill Christ's physical body on the cross, he only made his own situation worse. Three days later, Christ rose from the dead and for forty days appeared to the disciples. Then He ascended to heaven. About a week later, He began dwelling as the Holy Spirit in the apostles on that first Pentecost. Thus He became the living Word and the good news of the gospel of the kingdom dwelling in His Church. In a similar way, the two witnesses are only temporarily stopped. Christ is even now blowing His breath back into a remnant of the Church so they can get on their feet and once again spread the truth of the gospel. This time the entire world will be called to receive the Holy Spirit as the innumerable multitude. With this in mind, let's read Revelation 11:7-12. You will see a latter day event very similar to Christ's death, resurrection, and ascension into heaven: "When they finish their testimony, the beast that ascends out of the bottomless pit will make war against them, overcome them, and kill them. And their dead bodies will lie in the street of the great city which spiritually is called Sodom and Egypt, where also our Lord was crucified. Then those from the peoples, tribes, tongues, and nations will see their dead bodies three-and-a-half days, and not allow their dead bodies to be put into graves. And those who dwell on the earth will rejoice over them, make merry, and send gifts to one another, because these two prophets tormented those who dwell on the earth. Now after the three-and-a-half days the breath of life from God entered them, and they stood on their feet, and great fear fell on those who saw them. And they heard a loud voice from heaven saying to them, 'Come up here.' And they ascended to heaven in a cloud, and their enemies saw them."

Unlocking a Few More Mysteries

Instead of viewing certain mysterious symbols in Revelation as massive physical wars in the last days, we can now understand how God was warning His Church about spiritual warfare at the end. Christ was warning His Church that they would face the demonic realm in a difficult end-time battle unlike any that had ever been fought before. Let's look at a few examples of how God's intentions were to reveal spiritual battles instead of physical.

1.) The locusts of Revelation 9 are not picturing any sort of modern weaponry, but rather Satan's army that has been plaguing the Church for two thousand years (Revelation 9:1-3 and 11-12): "Then the fifth angel sounded: And I saw a star fallen from heaven to the earth. To him was given the key to the bottomless pit. And he opened the bottomless pit, and smoke arose out of the pit like the smoke of a great furnace. So the sun and the air were darkened because of the smoke of the pit. Then out of the smoke locusts came upon the earth. And to them was given power, as the scorpions of the earth have power... And they had as king over them the angel of the bottomless pit, whose name in Hebrew is Abaddon, but in Greek he has the name Apollyon. One woe is past. Behold, still two more woes are coming after these things." These locusts are mentioned in the Book of Joel 1:1-7 as spiritual beings that attack God's garden and His woman, the Church: "The word of the Lord that came to Joel the son of Pethuel. Hear this, you elders, and give ear, all you inhabitants of the land! Has anything like this happened in your days, or even in the days of your fathers? Tell your children about it, let your children tell their children, and their children another generation. What the chewing locust left, the swarming locust has eaten; what the swarming locust left, the crawling locust has eaten; and what the crawling locust left, the consuming locust has eaten. Awake, you drunkards, and weep; and wail, all you drinkers of wine, because of the new wine, for it has been cut off from your mouth. For a nation has come up against My land, strong, and without number; his teeth are the teeth of a lion, and he has the fangs of a fierce lion. He has laid waste My vine, and ruined My fig tree; he has stripped it bare and thrown it away; its branches are made white."

2.) The physical armies of the earth are not going to gather in the Middle East, but rather Satan and his demons will be brought together at the Battle of Armageddon to face Christ, His angels, and His resurrected saints. Armageddon is a symbolic name mentioned only in Revelation 16:16 (#717 Strong 1995), which is a combination of two Hebrew words from the Old Testament: *Har* #2022 and *Megiddown* #4023. *Har* means "a mountain or range of hills (sometimes used figuratively)," and *Meggiddown* means a rendezvous or a place in Palestine. This battle at Har-Megiddo is literally a rendezvous with destiny, which is what Har-Megiddo means in Hebrew. We can read about this battle in Revelation 16 verses 12-16: "Then the sixth angel poured out his bowl on the great river Euphrates, and its water was dried up, so that the way of the kings from the east might be prepared. And I saw three unclean spirits like frogs coming out of the mouth of the dragon, out of the mouth of the beast, and out of the mouth of the false prophet. For they are spirits of demons, performing signs, which go out to the kings of the earth and of the whole world, to gather them to the battle of that great day of God Almighty. 'Behold, I am coming as a thief. Blessed is he who watches, and keeps his garments, lest he walk naked and they see his shame.' And they gathered them together to the place called in Hebrew, Armageddon." Now let's cross reference Armageddon with Revelation 9:13-18. Keep in mind these Scriptures are part of the messages to the seven churches. They describe the Church's battles against Satan's realm, with particular focus on the great spiritual battle over spiritual Jerusalem and Mount Zion (Hebrews 12:18-24).

We can almost picture a spiritual battle in the heavens when we read of this great battle in Isaiah 31 verses 4-5: "For thus the Lord has spoken to me: 'As a lion roars, and a young lion over his prey (when a multitude of shepherds is summoned against him, he will not be afraid of their voice nor be disturbed by their noise), so the Lord of Hosts will come down to fight for Mount Zion and for its hill. Like birds flying about, so will the Lord of Host defend

Jerusalem. Defending, He will also deliver it; passing over, He will preserve it.'" Instead of envisioning a horrible physical battle on earth, we can now picture the time when Satan's realm will come crashing down and God's kingdom will become reality.

For a brief time, the river of life slowed to a trickle as Satan seemed to gain the upper hand. Christ said in John 7:38, "He who believes in Me, as the Scripture has said, out of his heart will flow rivers of living water." The physical parallel of this spiritual river is the Euphrates, the river that first flowed into the Garden of Eden. Euphrates in Hebrew is *perath* meaning "to break forth; rushing... a river of the east" (#6578 Strong 1995). A second definition for Euphrates is *parah* meaning "to bear fruit, literally or figuratively" (#6509 Strong 1995). In the New Testament the word Euphrates (#2166 Strong 1995) is a derivation of several words:

euphraino - "to put... in a good frame of mind, i.e. rejoice" (#2165 Strong 1995)

euphoreo - "to bear well, i.e. be fertile" (#2164 Strong 1995)

eupheus - "well spoken" (#2163 Strong 1995)

euphemia - "good language... i.e. praise" (#2162 Strong 1995)

The prefix *eu* (#2095 Strong 1995) means good, well done.

Soon the trickle will become a huge river healing the whole world (Revelation 22:1-2), and God will once again say as He did in Genesis 1 verse 31: "Then God saw everything that He had made, and indeed it was very good."

14
Mountains Fall, Mountains Rise

We studied the great image of Nebuchadnezzar's dream. We compared Daniel 2 to Daniel 10 and learned that Satan has divided the earth into principalities governed by his demon cohorts in a manner reflected upon the earth – a shadow of his government's image above. We also noticed that a stone cut out without human hands would smite the image at its feet, causing it to collapse in a heap and be blown away. Let's reread Daniel 2 verses 31-35: "You, O king, were watching; and behold, a great image! This great image, whose splendor was excellent, stood before you; and its form was awesome. This image's head was of fine gold, its chest and arms of silver, its belly and thighs of bronze, its legs of iron, its feet partly of iron and partly of clay. You watched while a stone was cut out without hands, which struck the image on its feet of iron and clay, and broke them in pieces. Then the iron, the clay, the bronze, the silver, and the gold were crushed together, and became like chaff from the summer threshing floors; the wind carried them away so that no trace of them was found. And the stone that struck the image became a great mountain and filled the whole earth."

The main import of this dream is a timeline leading right to our day and age. God's overall government is pictured as a mountain which will fill the whole earth. Do not look for a super Mount Everest to grow and consume the whole globe! This is a spiritual mountain which will replace Satan's government (a government also portrayed as a mountain right in your Bible). It is the spiritual mountain Christ was taken up on when He was tempted by Satan in Matthew 4:8-11. This was a titanic struggle for the future of mankind: "Again, the devil took Him up on an exceedingly high mountain, and showed Him all the kingdoms of the world and their glory. And he said to Him, 'All these things I will give You if You will fall down and worship me.' Then Jesus said to him, 'Away with you, Satan! For it is written, "You shall worship the Lord your God, and Him only you shall serve."' Then the devil left Him, and behold, angels came and ministered to Him." That is the event which gave the beast (and by extension his image) its mortal wound in Revelation 13:3. It is a wound which will prove fatal to Satan's system very soon.

Now we will cross reference this evil mountain of Satan's in the Old Testament. We discover that it has a name in Scripture in Ezekiel 35 verses 1-9: "Moreover the word of the Lord came to me, saying, 'Son of man, set your face against Mount Seir and prophesy against it, and say to it, "Thus says the Lord God: 'Behold, O Mount Seir, I am against you; I will stretch out My hand against you, and make you most desolate; I shall lay your cities waste, and you shall be desolate. Then you shall know that I am the Lord. Because you have had an ancient hatred, and have shed the blood of the children of Israel by the power of the sword at the time of their calamity, when their iniquity came to an end, therefore, as I live,' says the Lord God, 'I will prepare you for blood, and blood shall pursue you; since you have not hated blood [bloodshed], therefore blood shall pursue you. Thus I will make Mount Seir most desolate, and cut off from it the one who leaves and the one who returns. And I will fill its mountains with the slain; on your hills and in your valleys and in all your ravines those who are slain by the sword shall fall. I will make you perpetually desolate, and your cities shall be uninhabited; then you shall know that I am the Lord.'"'"

In these verses, God is painting a vivid picture of the fall of Satan's chief mountain and his entire mountain range that sits astride the earth. Mount Seir in Hebrew means the mountain of the rough shaggy he-goat, a devil, which causes mankind to shiver in fear. That is the meaning of the word Seir.

Satan made war on God's people in the Old Testament (the first chosen nation or *ekklesia*), for he wanted to stop the prophets who gave their lives to lay the foundation of the prophets (their prophetic words of truth). He wanted to destroy their temple, their statutes, and the systems God gave them to enact physically so that we could comprehend what He is now doing in a spiritual way.

This mountain and its mountain chain have had an ancient hatred for God and all that God stands for. In this prophecy God warns Satan that since he has pushed mankind to bloodshed, by the blood of man He will destroy his government and its power. No more will Satan and his emissaries come and go and trample upon the earth and its people. By God's sword (the word of God) he will be laid desolate. As mankind accepts the blood of Christ and becomes converted, blood shall be removed from Satan's sphere of influence. Flesh and blood shall no longer be his dwelling place. As more people get converted, the weaker Satan will become! It all started with the blood of one Man first, Jesus Christ.

Understanding prophecies such as these allay our anxieties and fear and give us confidence in our Almighty God. Jeremiah 51:25-26 repeats God's threat to Satan's mountain: "'Behold, I am against you, O destroying mountain, who destroys all the earth,' says the Lord. 'And I will stretch out My hand against you, roll you down from the rocks, and make you a burnt mountain. They shall not take from you a stone for a corner nor a stone for a foundation, but you shall be desolate forever,' says the Lord."

God is not angry with physical mountain chains on the earth. He hates what they currently represent. He is angry with the beings who laid waste, conquered, and pillaged His beautiful creation and the human race which He created in His own image.

To picture Satan's kingdom in your mind, view the earth as ringed with dark mountains, chief of which is Mount Seir. It would look similar to a day with dark clouds above, towering in the sky like mighty mountains shading the earth and keeping the light of the sun away from the earth. It would be like watching the shadow of a cloud move across the landscape. These mountains block God's light causing darkness. On the chief of these mountains sits Satan's capital city, spiritual Babylon, from which he sends out his mighty horsemen, the four horsemen of the Apocalypse, to stir up mankind against one another.

The earth is divided into spheres of influence under Satan's demons. These spiritual tyrants come and go from the capital Babylon to the earth wreaking havoc. Let's put together a string of Scriptures to back up this understanding.

- Isaiah 14:3-4, 12-15 "It shall come to pass in the day the Lord gives you rest from your sorrow [brings us the Millennium of peace] and from your fear and the hard bondage in which you were made to serve, that you will take up this proverb against the king of Babylon, and say: 'How the oppressor has ceased, the golden city ceased!'" Verse 12: "How you are fallen from heaven, O Lucifer, son of the morning! How you are cut down to the ground, you who weakened the nations! For you have said in your heart: 'I will ascend into heaven, I will exalt my throne above the stars of God; I will also sit on the mount of the congregation on the farthest sides of the north; I will ascend above the heights of the clouds, I will be like the Most High.' Yet you shall be brought down to Sheol, to the lowest depths of the pit."

- Ephesians 6:12 "For we do not wrestle against flesh and blood, but against principalities, against powers, against the rulers of the darkness of this age, against spiritual hosts of wickedness in the heavenly places."

- Revelation 18:2 Of this Babylon it will soon be said, "And he cried mightily with a loud voice, saying, 'Babylon the great is fallen, is fallen, and has become a dwelling place of demons, a prison for every foul spirit, and a cage for every unclean and hated bird!'"

- Revelation 17:5-6, 18 "And on her forehead a name was written: MYSTERY, BABYLON THE GREAT, THE MOTHER OF HARLOTS AND OF THE ABOMINATIONS OF THE EARTH. I saw the woman, drunk with the blood of the saints and with the blood of the martyrs of Jesus. And when I saw her, I marveled with great amazement." Verse 18: "And the woman whom you saw is that great city which reigns over the kings of the earth."

Babylon, the name of this capital city, means bitterness, confusion, wormwood, calamity and tyranny. From this city, Satan has ruled in the affairs of mankind for six thousand years using peoples, empires and religions, anyone he could use to deceive mankind to try to stop God. All to no avail! God's victory is now imminent. For thousands of years men have uttered Psalm 23:4, and we can now more properly understand it: "Yea, though I walk through the valley of the shadow of death, I will fear no evil; for You are with me; Your rod and Your staff, they comfort me." Our existence has been in the valley between Satan's mountains under his capital city, the capital of the kingdom of darkness.

Just as light is the opposite of darkness, good is the opposite of evil. So God's kingdom will be the opposite of Satan's realm. Satan's principalities and the powers over them will be replaced by God's government. It will be a government based on mercy, compassion, and the light of the truth. It will be a government that brings peace. Instead of pulling people down, it will lift them up. Instead of appealing to the baser instincts of lust, greed, and fierce competition, it will appeal to our desires for kindness, cooperation and respect for the dignity of each and every human being. We will let God speak to us about this wonderful period of time just ahead. We will let Scripture paint the picture for us in our minds.

- Isaiah 2:2-4 "Now it shall come to pass in the latter days that the mountain of the Lord's house shall be established on the top of the mountains, and shall be exalted above the hills; and all nations shall flow to it. Many people shall come and say, 'Come, and let us go up to the mountain of the Lord, to the house of the God of Jacob; He will teach us His ways, and we shall walk in His paths.' For out of Zion shall go forth the law, and the word of the Lord from Jerusalem. He shall judge between the nations, and rebuke many people; they shall beat their swords into plowshares, and their spears into pruning hooks; nation shall not lift up sword against nation, neither shall they learn war anymore."

- Isaiah 11:6-9 "The wolf also shall dwell with the lamb, the leopard shall lie down with the young goat, the calf and the young lion and the fatling together; and a little child shall lead them. The cow and the bear shall graze; their young ones shall lie down together; and the lion shall eat straw like the ox. The nursing child shall play by the cobra's hole, and the weaned child shall put his hand in the viper's den. They shall not hurt nor destroy in all My holy mountain, for the earth shall be full of the knowledge of the Lord as the waters cover the sea."

It is evident that God's truth will wipe out the ignorance and the darkness which now plague mankind. God's truth is indeed the knowledge that will set us free from the weaknesses Satan exploits to divide, conquer and destroy. God's influence (His voice) will cover the earth, as well as replace the influence of the little voice we now hear that tells us so often, "Don't get mad, get even." "Go ahead and take it. They will never miss it." "Lie your way out of it. Don't let yourself look bad." "It's okay to do that person bodily harm because they are a different color. They are a different religion. They are a different nationality."

This kind of broadcast by the current ruler of this world will be replaced with a good voice as shown in Isaiah 30 verse 21: "Your ears shall hear a word behind you, saying, 'This is the way, walk in it,' whenever you turn to the right hand or whenever you turn to the left." God's voice, His Holy Spirit, and His knowledge will permeate the earth and all life upon it. It will direct us. When we tend to veer off the straight and narrow a voice will tell us, "please behave and do what is right." Even the nature of the animals will be changed! All of this will emanate from His spiritual mountains, His spiritual capital city, and will be reflected on the earth.

Physical Jerusalem will still exist on the earth and will be a city of peace and a physical example of God's way of life. But above will be a spiritual Jerusalem which will be the actual source of the peace that will be shed abroad upon the earth. The power behind all of these wonderful changes will come from God's spiritual mountain in that city, a shining city. It will be a city on the mountains surrounded by the hills. They will be like the clouds now surrounding the earth that block the sun, but these hills will be sources of the truth. Instead of blocking the light of truth, they will bring it to mankind. Remember that truth and doctrine are like rain to the earth. There is a saying that rain is merely liquid sunshine, and so it will be!

This beautiful spiritual city will reign from above for one thousand years, just as Satan's city ruled for six thousand. At the end of that Millennium it will descend to earth as we are told in Revelation 21. This will make earth the center of the universe forever after!

Let's turn to a few more Scriptures to finish painting this beautiful picture for us. Turn to Hebrews 12:18, 22-23 which speaks volumes to us to help us understand these things: "For you have not come to the mountain that may be touched and that burned with fire, and to blackness and darkness and tempest..." Verse 22: "But you have come to Mount Zion and to the city of the living God, the heavenly Jerusalem, to an innumerable company of angels, to the general assembly and church of the firstborn who are registered in heaven, to God the Judge of all, to the spirits of just men made perfect..."

These "just men made perfect" are the dead saints in Christ, the firstfruit harvest, the few who have given their lives for the many. Galatians 4:25-26 refers to this spiritual city in this way: "...for this Hagar is Mount Sinai in Arabia, and corresponds to Jerusalem which now is, and is in bondage with her children but the Jerusalem above is free, which is the mother of us all." Just as spiritual Babylon is depicted as a vile woman, a mother of harlots, so spiritual Jerusalem is depicted as the mother of the firstfruits and eventually the mother of all! It will be a mother to all who live on into the Millennium and all of those who have died and who will be resurrected. God intends to win big! He is in no way a minimalist.

Our marvelous future now explodes off the pages of the

Bible as we read and understand such Scriptures as Isaiah 66 verses 6-13: "The sound of noise from the city! A voice from the temple! The voice of the Lord, who fully repays His enemies! 'Before she was in labor, she gave birth; before her pain came, she delivered a male child. Who has heard such a thing? Who has seen such things? Shall the earth be made to give birth in one day? Or shall a nation be born at once? For as soon as Zion was in labor, she gave birth to her children. Shall I bring to the time of birth, and not cause delivery?' says the Lord. 'Shall I who cause delivery shut up the womb?' says your God. 'Rejoice with Jerusalem, and be glad with her, all you who love her; rejoice for joy with her, all you who mourn for her; that you may feed and be satisfied with the consolation of her bosom, that you may drink deeply and be delighted with the abundance of her glory.' For thus says the Lord; 'Behold, I will extend peace to her like a river, and the glory of the Gentiles like a flowing stream. Then you shall feed; on her sides shall you be carried, and be dandled on her knees. As one whom his mother comforts, so I will comfort you; and you shall be comforted in Jerusalem.'" It is truly amazing! God is letting you understand now because these things are so close to becoming reality!

God will soon use every tool at His disposal to stamp out darkness, ignorance, and evil influence. He will use His sword, the word of God, the Bible, (Hebrews 4:12). He will use the wind and the breath of His mouth (His Holy Spirit) to blow the image away (Daniel 2 and John 3). Christ will make His blood available for all. Christ will make the true signs and wonders known to everyone on earth, and the knowledge of what creation represents will be brought upon the earth as the sea covers earth now! That is clearly stated in Romans 1 verses 18-20: "For the wrath of God is revealed from heaven against all ungodliness and unrighteousness of men, who suppress the truth in unrighteousness, because what may be known of God is manifest in them, for God has shown it to them. For since the creation of the world His invisible attributes are clearly seen, being understood by the things that are made, even His eternal power and Godhead, so that they are without excuse..."

When God decides to reveal His truth, it is not a good time to willingly stay ignorant or deny it. God has been working on this plan for a long time, and is very excited to have arrived at this juncture. Titus 1:1-3 explains that God made promises to mankind and a plan to keep those promises before time began: "Paul, a bondservant of God and an apostle of Jesus Christ, according to the faith of God's elect and the acknowledgment of the truth which accords with godliness, in hope of eternal life which God, who cannot lie, promised before time began, but has in due time manifested His word through preaching, which was committed to me according to the commandment of God our Savior..."

God is putting mankind on notice regarding a number of things. (1) Do not stand in His way by teaching doctrines of waste and destruction which are false signs and wonders (Matthew 24:4-8). (2) He warns oppressors and tyrants to stop allowing themselves to be tools of Satan. Care for your people's physical needs, and promote an atmosphere of freedom to learn of God (Proverbs 28:15-16). (3) He warns all governments to pursue peace and to promote human rights and dignity of all human beings (Proverbs 20:28). (4) He tells the rich and the powerful to care for the less fortunate (II Corinthians 9:6-7). (5) To all people everywhere He says forgive one another and lay aside your differences, for by forgiveness we take away Satan's power to incite hatred, animosity and violence (Matthew 6:14 and Luke 6:37). (6) To all people everywhere God says love your neighbor as yourself (Matthew 22:39, and the story of the Good Samaritan in Luke 10:25-37). (7) Love and obey God on His terms. Matthew 22 verses 37-38: "Jesus said to him, 'You shall love the Lord your God with all your heart, with all your soul, and with all your mind. This is the first and great commandment.'" Again Christ says in John 14:15-16, "If you love Me, keep My commandments. And I will pray the Father, and He will give you another Helper, that He may abide with you forever..."

We now live in the time foreordained by God eons ago to be a turning point in the battle between good and evil. There are a number of ways we can assist Him and our fellow man at this defining moment. The following key ways will get the light of the truth glowing brightly and help defeat the forces of darkness. First, start by obeying all of God's commandments, for by obedience we gain wisdom and understanding. His commandments teach us to love God above all else, and next to love our fellow man who was made in His image. With obedience, understanding will flood into our minds. Exercising forgiveness is a critical step in weakening Satan's power.

This is a great time to be alive! The dawn of a new age is just over the horizon. With a little spiritual vision and insight, we can see its first rays begin to illuminate the eastern sky. Soon all eyes will see Jesus Christ coming in power and glory, and we will finally be able to hold our heads up as a human race, set free from tyranny and oppression.

Satan inspires division, hatred, racism, lust, and greed. God in His truth inspires love, mercy, compassion, and forgiveness. These are the powers of light which disarm Satan and free us! These are the powers that will teach us to end war and violence, fulfilling Isaiah 2 verse 4: "He shall judge between nations, and rebuke many people; they shall beat their swords into plowshares, and their spears into pruning hooks; nation shall not lift up sword against nation, neither shall they learn war anymore." One cannot over-estimate the power of forgiveness to heal this planet. The unleashing of this power will destroy Satan's influence.

Satan has spent the last six thousand years dividing families, pitting nation against nation, kingdom against kingdom, civilization against civilization. The current distress among nations can and will be the end of Satan's influence. In the past economic turmoil, greed, and lust for power have resulted in wars, famines, oppression, and more tyranny - all expressions of Satan's influence.

Satan is the "prince of the power of the air" (Ephesians 2:2), constantly broadcasting his evil thoughts and temptation into the minds of human beings. All too often we have been compliant to his desires, letting him dictate the course of our lives. Our minds operate like radio receivers, tuned to hear his broadcasts telling us to take offense, hold grudges, and lash back. The little voice says,

"Don't get mad, get even," or better yet, "Get mad and get even."

In this day and age, Satan has more avenues into our minds than ever before. Television, radio, movies, Internet, and video games push his agenda of violence, perversion, lust, and greed. These devices give the forces of darkness the ability to flood the world with the state of his mind, the evil hiss of their breath.

There is much we can personally do to turn down the hiss of the demon world and counter the downward pull of his influence. We have the choice to turn off electronic devices or to change channels. Nobody can force us to sit in a darkened theater and view evil. Nobody can force us to watch dogs fight, cocks fight, or humans pummel each other in a ring or cage. Nobody can force us to buy violent video games for our children. Nobody can force us to strap a bomb around our waist or the waist of a child to maim and kill.

We have the incomparable gift of free will. We need to use it. We must choose to use it wisely and for good. Revelation 7:9 tells us that soon, "a great multitude which no one could number, of all nations, tribes, peoples, and tongues..." will have made the right choice. In verse 14 the angel tells John, "These are the ones who came out of the great tribulation, and washed their robes and made them white in the blood of the Lamb." Great tribulation does not mean enormous death and destruction. This is a great tribulation because so many choose the way of the gospel and determine to fight the good fight in their minds and hearts. Satan's death grip on earth weakens with every conversion to the gospel of the kingdom. The times and seasons are changing. Seeds of the kingdom have been planted all over the earth. The Bible has been published in huge quantities. Due to the hard work and sacrifices of many people, the word of God has been translated into almost every language and dialect. It has been distributed worldwide, and more people than ever before are free to read it. Truly dramatic changes for the good lie just ahead.

Things are different today. Around the world the heartbeat of hope is beating stronger and stronger. Almost unnoticed, peace has broken out in Northern Ireland. China has renounced the first use of nuclear weapons. Libya has dismantled its machinery of war. More people around the earth have come out of poverty in the last twenty-five years than in the history of the world. Non-government organizations (NGO's) and philanthropists vow to eradicate AIDs, malaria, and hunger. Once-mortal enemies trade goods and services instead of bullets and bombs. Nearly the entire world is working together to stabilize the world's economic system and basic human rights. We have come a long way toward making the family of man less dysfunctional. Forgiveness is the key to success. Forgive debts and forgive offenses. If we use Christ's model prayer as a pattern for our supplications to God and if we each practice it in our lives, the fruits of God's kingdom can be growing and spreading right now. Matthew 6 verses 9-15: "In this manner, therefore, pray: Our Father in heaven, hallowed be Your name. Your kingdom come. Your will be done on earth as it is in heaven. Give us this day our daily bread. And forgive us our debts, as we forgive our debtors. And do not lead us into temptation, but deliver us from the evil one. For Yours is the kingdom and the power and the glory forever. Amen. For if you forgive men their trespasses, your heavenly Father will also forgive you. But if you do not forgive men their trespasses, neither will your Father forgive your trespasses."

We can all learn to forgive offenses and stop carrying grudges. We can all share our physical blessings with the less fortunate. Wherever we see need, do something to relieve burdens. Be fair in business. Work hard at our jobs. Pay our bills. Forgive a debt to those who struggle whenever the opportunity arises - realizing that it is an opportunity. Living the way of "give" versus "get" will put us on the right side of history. The impact of doing good will grow and compound across the earth. The soon-coming kingdom of God will give us a great deal of freedom to develop and use our personal talents and abilities. The unifying effect of all humanity living by God's laws will be astounding. Instead of living by a patchwork quilt of competing religions and denominations, we will honor God as He has set forth in His holy word. This new reality will not be confining. It will be wonderfully liberating!

Embracing the Future

The current distress among nations is palpably perplexing to literally everyone. Nobody seems to have the answers to the debt crisis, falling stock markets, home foreclosures, and job losses. Thousands of experts weigh in with many ideas for "fixing" the world's ills. These well-meaning people want to offer helpful advice and suggestions, but they do not understand the real forces at work. Here is a sampling of what you are probably hearing:

- save the banks through recaptialization
- buy gold
- invest in oil
- sell your stocks
- buy stocks now while prices are down
- stock up on food
- walk away from debt violations
- invest in foreign currencies
- inflation is the enemy
- deflation is the great threat

All this confusion in the world today calls to mind a prophecy of our time in Luke 21:25-26 which is a part of Christ's response to His disciples' query as to signs of the end and His return: "And there will be signs in the sun, in the moon, and in the stars; and on the earth distress of nations, with perplexity, the sea and the waves roaring; men's hearts failing them from fear and the expectation of those things which are coming on the earth, for the powers of the heavens will be shaken."

Do not let the prophets of doom use these words to cause you to be fearful or anxious. Many, for their own profit or egotistical satisfaction, are using Christ's words falsely. In Luke 21:28 Christ specifically says to "Look up and lift your heads, because your redemption draws near."

You find yourself alive at the time for which mankind has been waiting for six thousand years - the end of Satan's reign. "The waves roaring" is simply the sea of mankind crying for help while in a state of confusion. You need not be perplexed, for just like those who heard Peter explain the true signs and wonders on that first Pentecost, you now know what is really going on. Satan's heavenly realm is convulsing as his power wanes and his hills and mountains collapse. His influence that led mankind to build an image of Satan's system on earth, based on greed, avarice, and corruption is changing in a final spiritual battle. The battle is Armageddon for Satan's way of life.

In the past Armageddon was a place of physical war, but today it is a rendezvous with destiny when Satan's mountains and hills clash with God's. It is the time when Satan's power and influence come to an end. It is a great time to be alive! It is a time when the world's people can lift their heads in liberty.

What It Will Be Like

The world is transitioning into a different way of life. From a distance earth will look the same - a beautiful blue jewel with puffy white clouds. But unlike today on this earth, peace will have replaced war. Man's imagination and intellect will turn away from inventing machines to wage war. Trillions of dollars, rubles, yen, euros, and yuan will be spent productively. Clean renewable energy will be used on a vast scale. The poor, the homeless, and the oppressed will be cared for and given opportunity.

Yes: there will be banks
Yes: there will be stock markets
Yes: there will be big business
Yes: there will be small business

But the way of "give" will replace "get." Intense competition of a dog-eat-dog world will be replaced with cooperation. If you look into today's news, you can already see these trends growing in the human race. The beautiful wind of God's Holy Spirit is already blowing across the earth. A fractured human race is becoming the family of man. No longer will the earth bear the image of Satan. God's intended purpose of making mankind into His image and likeness will have become a reality. It will have been accomplished with mankind's cooperation. When knowledge of God replaces ignorance, the vast majority of the human race will choose good over evil.

Do not fear the future. Embrace it, for the end of tyranny is almost here. Currently that august body known as the United Nations is often ridiculed, scorned, ignored, and even laughed at. However, what the United Nations represents is man's attempt to unshackle himself from war, poverty, and disease. These are noble goals that will be achieved very soon. What has held mankind back are the dark influences that echo in the minds of human beings. Those influences have caused remembrance of offenses long past and rekindled grudges, making millstones around our necks. Those evil influences have divided, politicized, and corrupted the best efforts of the human race.

Soon we will be set free from evil influence, not because almost all of us have physically perished in a cataclysmic end, but rather because the earth will know the true God. "They shall not hurt nor destroy in all My holy mountain, for the earth shall be full of the knowledge of the Lord as the waters cover the sea" (Isaiah 11:9).

Then the chambers of the United Nations will be full of the sounds of the family of man solving problems together and planning for the future. Around the world will echo the sounds of men beating swords into plowshares. Jerusalem will really be a city of peace and truly a guiding light to the world. The sweet and peaceful influences of a spiritual Jerusalem above will reverberate in the hearts and minds of men for one thousand years. The symbols of the United Nations will have become reality!

If you would like to join the effort to make this book available to all who request it, your help is certainly appreciated.

Great Lakes Church of God
P.O. Box 1272
Aberdeen, NC 28315
U.S.A.
Learn more at
www.TheBeautifulThoughtsOfGod.com

Index